THE STORY OF THE STORIES

THE STORY OF THE STORIES

The Chosen People and Its God

DAN JACOBSON

HARPER & ROW, PUBLISHERS, New York

Cambridge, Philadelphia, San Francisco, London,
Mexico City, São Paulo, Sydney

1817

FIRST EDITION

Designer: Sidney Feinberg

Library of Congress Cataloging in Publication Data

Jacobson, Dan.
   The story of the stories.
   Bibliography: p.
   1. Jews—History—To 70 A.D.   2. Bible—History of
Biblical events.   I. Title.
DS118.J23   221.9'5   81–48154
ISBN 0–06–014986–8   AACR2

---

82 83 84 85 86 10 9 8 7 6 5 4 3 2 1

CONTENTS

ACKNOWLEDGMENTS

If true, not new; if new, not true. The Bible has been examined more devotedly, and over a longer period, than any other document in existence. Much of what follows will be familiar to readers with a special interest in the subject. There would be something seriously amiss with this work (and with me) if that were not the case. However, I hope there is enough that is both new and true in my treatment of the themes of choice and chosenness to attract readers of all kinds.

The book has been written as a kind of narrative, in a spirit of critical speculation; not as a work of scholarship. I have no scholarly knowledge of the languages in which the Scriptures were originally written, and have been dependent on translations throughout. But I have learned sufficient Hebrew to be able to use with interest and pleasure the parallel Hebrew-English texts of the Pentateuch, and of some of the prophetic books, published by the Soncino Press (London, Jerusalem, New York). The few references I make to the original Hebrew are from this source.

All biblical quotations (except for the epigraph, which is from the Authorized Version) are taken from the Revised Standard Version. Acknowledgments are due to the Prince-

viii   ACKNOWLEDGMENTS

ton University Press for permission to quote in Chapter Five an extract from the translation of the treaty between Esarhaddon and Ramataya which appears in *The Ancient Near Eastern Texts Relating to the Old Testament*, edited by James B. Pritchard. Other works which I have found helpful are listed in the Select Bibliography appearing at the end of the book. In each case I have simply cited the edition which was most readily available to me. It is from these editions that all quotations appearing in the text have been taken.

I would like to thank Susan Oldacre and Hilary Clark, of the English Department, University College London, for their patient and skillful secretarial help with various versions of this book; and Rosemary Ashton, Ian Hamilton, Aaron Klug, and Ann Molan, for comments they made on sections shown to them in draft form. I am obliged, too, to Ted Solotaroff and Marjorie Horvitz of Harper & Row for their help with the manuscript.

D.J.

Now therefore, if ye will obey my voice indeed, and keep my covenant, then ye shall be a peculiar treasure unto me above all people: for all the earth is mine.

EXODUS 19:5

THE STORY OF THE STORIES

INTRODUCTION

To many people the God who was revealed to the ancient Israelites remains what he has always been: the creator of the universe, the source of all life, the arbiter of the destinies of men and nations. To others the God of Israel is a fiction, a figure from a wholly discredited myth or series of myths, part of a primitive system of belief which has long outlived its purpose and which it is now impossible to take seriously.

In this book I do intend to take the God of ancient Israel seriously, in the only way I can: *as* a fiction, as a fantasy, as an imaginative creation. My aim is to try to understand the relationship presented in the Scriptures between the people of Israel and the God they had created; and to follow through to an end (so far as it has one) the "plot" in which God and people were reciprocally engaged. My hope is to learn from this something about the moral imagination and its connections with our fantasy life. My approach is that of a novelist, of a writer and reader of fictions. However, so far from wishing the reader to consider the narrative in some kind of formalistic or aesthetic vacuum, I want him constantly to keep in mind that it is the record of a passionately held and militant faith.

The faith is not one that I share, or have ever shared.

(Though I was brought up to be conscious of my identity as a Jew, my home background was almost entirely a secular one.) In a sense, that is exactly what has attracted me to the idea of examining, in the terms I have just stated, the tale outlined above. The God of Israel is presented in a narrative, or through a narrative, which because of its very nature appears to be more accessible to the nonbeliever than any set of doctrines or dogma could be. By examining it, and the variety of ways in which it is told, the skeptic should be able to get a grasp, which would otherwise elude him, of at least one aspect of a history which has been continuous from ancient times to the present day. Within obvious limitations, he may also be able to gain a greater comprehension than before of the faith of his forebears, as well as of the faith of those among his contemporaries, whether they be Jews or Gentiles, who look to the Bible for divine guidance and revelation. Like any other work of criticism and speculation, this book must justify itself by the persuasiveness of its arguments; on that level, my motives in writing it are of no relevance whatever. But it may help the reader to get his bearings in what follows if, among other things, he sees it as an attempt by the writer to make contact with a tradition from which he has always felt himself sundered, and which has yet affected his life, and the life of everyone around him, in more ways than he can possibly enumerate.

The essential subject of this book is the dramatic tensions within the overarching myth or legend of a people chosen by an all-powerful God to serve his purposes. It is in that legend that all the historical and biographical narratives of the Hebrew Bible, and all its laws and prophecies, are embedded. If Yahweh is wholly a human creation, as I believe him to be, then his actions and the utterances ascribed to him in his dealings with his people must reveal needs and fears which his creators could express in no other way. The fact that they did not believe him to be their creation, but on the contrary believed themselves to be *his* creation, does not necessarily alter the moral and psychological processes involved as much as might be supposed.

We take it for granted that any story which enthralls us, from a little fairy tale like "Cinderella" to a great tragedy like *Oedipus the King*, owes some of its power to hidden or obscured elements which help to determine the direction it takes; we assume that we are entitled to look for these, and to make them explicit, in trying to understand its overall effect. It is on that assumption that I want to explore "the story of the stories" told in the Hebrew Scriptures. I might add in passing, and without wishing to be facetious, that the tale of Cinderella—which is largely about someone who is despised and passed over, and who then turns out to be chosen for love and preeminence, while others who had prided themselves on their position are cast into darkness—has a certain resemblance to what follows. An acknowledgment of the appetite we feel for narratives of all kinds, and a sympathetic regard for the elements which are common to them all, must bring us closer to understanding why the imperious invention of an omnipotent God and his chosen people should have proved to be one of the most compelling and also one of the most catastrophic in human history.

The stories we know best have a clear beginning and end; they are graspable by the mind in what seems to be a single act of apprehension; they usually come to us as the invention of one person who has set himself a particular task, and carried it through to a conclusion. The Hebrew

Scriptures, by contrast, are an elaborately assembled library or compendium of works of different kinds, many of them drawing on legends, oral histories, and cultic practices of immemorial antiquity; all of them written, revised, and collated over a period of about a thousand years by an unknown multitude of hands. Is it really possible to extract from such an assemblage a coherent if equivocal story or drama, exactly as if it were a single text, the expression of an identifiable point of view—a "work," in short?

Obviously I think it is; and I am far from being alone in thinking so. For most of the time it has been in existence, readers of the Bible have taken its essential unity for granted. For century after century people had no difficulty in basing their interpretations of it upon what seemed to them this self-evident fact. "Oh, but they believed it was all true!" a skeptical reader might object. Well, some did; some did not. But they all recognized—they did not invent—the accumulating parallels, echoes, internal allusions, inversions, and almost obsessive reworkings and rewordings of important themes and problems in the major historical and prophetic books. And, of course, in the Christian Scriptures, too. One does not have to believe in the literal veracity of these books, or even hold some more elaborate theory about their divine provenance, as most modern biblical scholars appear to do, in order to perceive these patterns, or to write about them. Nor need one deny, in doing so, that the books are astonishingly various in their strata, parts, and genres; that they are often simultaneously repetitive and self-contradictory; and that the disorder of their chronology is equaled only by their indifference to certain categories of logical thought which seem indispensable to us.

The fact is that at all their different stages, and in all their different forms, and with all their different emphases, the Scriptures reveal a continuous attempt by the writers and redactors to interpret in the terms bequeathed to them *by the text itself* everything that happened to them, and everything they hoped or feared might happen to their people in the future. It is precisely that attempt which confers upon the historical and prophetic books the unity—that is, the narrative continuity—they have. Changing political and cultural circumstances helped to determine the manner in which the writers conceived the God of Israel; nevertheless each of them firmly believed he was confronting the same God as the one his predecessors had spoken of: a God whose word and will, which all held to be eternal and unchanging, were to be fitted into and drawn out of any particular historical episode the writers were called on to celebrate or endure. Much the same can be said of their dealings with the other great protagonist in the drama: the people of Israel itself. Everyone who added anything to the compilation believed that the people he belonged to, the people whose history it was now his turn to narrate or to predict, and whose relationship with God it was now his turn to describe, was one family, descended in an unbroken line from Abraham. The land, too, whether it was won or lost, was seen as an unchanging promise or possession. So was the covenant between God and people. Because those who wrote and revised and ultimately canonized the Scriptures believed that they were participating in an eternal drama, they inevitably produced and handed on to succeeding generations the record of just such a drama. As in any drama worthy of the name, those involved in it try not only to respond to the actions of the other participants, but also to interpret these actions; they try to discern and declare, as best they can, the meanings of the entire experience they are compelled to undergo.

The central *donnée,* and hence the effective opening, of the biblical story is plain enough. It is the notion of a single transcendent God with a determining relationship to the history of one particular people, upon whom, from afar, he bestows a land. That is the relationship at the heart of its plot; or (to change the metaphor) that is the "gene" which controls the development of the entire system. Everything that happens within the story—which means everything that is reported to have happened to the people of Israel in the course of their history—is derived from this relationship and understood as a clarification or development of it. This is true even of the legends and myths and genealogies contained in Genesis. However ancient they may be, and they have the appearance of being very ancient indeed, they are clearly placed first in the text not because they achieved their written form first, or could in themselves explain what followed, but because what followed— or rather what was in some sense already "there"—demanded a series of prior explanations, and genealogies, and choices, which had to go back to the creation of the world.

At what particular stage the idea of the God of Israel became the possession of the people of Israel, or of a substantial part of the people, or of a decisive group within it, is a subject that is best left to the historians and theologians. All that matters here is that the text effectively knows no other God for the people of Israel: the traces of his predecessors, or his competitors, are so faint and rare as to be virtually indecipherable by the eye of the reader who has not been trained to look for them. To the historians and theologians, again, must be left the task of establishing if they can "what really happened" during the sojourn of the Israelites in the wilderness, say, or on the entry of the Israelites into Canaan; or when it happened; or how it happened; or to whom it happened; or indeed, whether or not any of it actually happened. I am interested in the story that was told, and went on being retold and elaborated upon, about a God who gave a land to the Israelites, and then punished them for their disobedience by taking the land from them: "events" which I am quite convinced never did happen.

The reader is entitled to know that my curiosity about the idea of the chosen people was sharpened or given a particular focus by an attempt to understand better some aspects of the great catastrophe which fell upon the Jews of Europe in the 1940s. Reading about the massacres, I was struck by how important a feature of the anti-Semitic propaganda of the Nazis was the alternatively menacing and consoling use they made of their versions of "chosenness." To the Jews they were ready to ascribe a total, active, malign confidence in their role as an elect group, convinced of their mission to lord it over all other nations, in the fullness (or nearness) of time. Simultaneously the Nazis declared themselves to be, as the representatives of the Aryan race, the people actually chosen by history to perform many great tasks, the most significant of these being that of ridding the world once for all of the Judaic menace hanging over it, and thus bringing about the millennium. (Quite literally the millennium: "the thousand-year Reich.")

These notions looked back in turn to publications like *The Protocols of the Elders of Zion*, in which obsessive ravings about the supposed schemes of the Jews to seize power worldwide and to enslave the *goyim* forever were justified by the assertion that the Jews were indeed a chosen people: chosen by Satan or the Antichrist as his own, and sent out into the world to do his bidding. And such obsessions looked back in their turn to two thousand years of central, indeed crucial, Christian teaching about how the children of Israel had forfeited their status as God's chosen people, through their failure to recognize Jesus as the Messiah, and had thus (in effect) become the children of Satan instead.

> They [the Jews] answered him, 'Abraham is our father.' Jesus said to them, 'If you were Abraham's children, you would do what Abraham did, but now you seek to kill me, a man who has told you the truth which I heard from God; this is not what Abraham did. You do what your father did . . . You are of your father the devil, and your will is to do your father's desires.'
>
> JOHN 8:39–41, 44

Since it was impossible, for historical, theological, and personal reasons, for the members of the new sect to repudiate the God of the Jews, they had to make sure that he did not appear to repudiate them. Paradoxically, it was the "Gentilization" of Christianity through the doctrines of Paul which, as we shall see, made this a matter of life and death for the Christians. If they were everything, the true or new elect, the real inheritors of the scriptural blessings, then their rivals to the patrimony had to be nothing—cast out, rejected, a negation of being—and to be seen as such by everybody else.

This is an ironic and fateful version of the pattern of choice and rejection, of *choice-as-rejection*, which is one of the central elements of the biblical drama to be discussed later. The fact that in the succeeding millennia the Jews nevertheless persisted in surviving as a distinctive group has been an everlasting provocation or "scandal" to most Christians: I suspect that for many of them it will always remain one.

Anyway, innumerable groups since then have believed themselves to be specially chosen not merely to fulfill an indispensable role within the course of history, but to give history the only meaning it has. Like the Israelites, especially those who were confronted with the catastrophes of conquest and dispossession, and who therefore looked forward with an ever-increasing intensity and grandiosity to some startling turn of events which would restore their fortunes, these latter-day chosen peoples have seen their collective fate as somehow providing the grand denouement or payoff to the otherwise pointless suffering that every human generation has to undergo. The Puritan settlers in America, for example, clearly believed themselves to be a people or "remnant" with a redemptive role of this kind; so did the members of the pan-Slav movement in Eastern Europe during the nineteenth century. The Marxists, it has often been said, have their own scheme of historical election and salvation, in which the revolutionary proletariat is assigned the task of bringing to an end history as the record of strife and exploitation it has hitherto been. The failure of the elect to accomplish this task—inside the Soviet bloc or outside it—has done as little to shake the Marxists out of their faith in the "scientific" veracity of their beliefs as the apparent hostility of their God has shaken Orthodox Jews out of the belief that he will eventually relent and show them a more benign face. That is how strongly men influenced by this tradition cling to the belief that history does not merely have a "plot," but also the promise of a happy ending—for some; that is how difficult they find it to accept the possibility that the miseries of human history may be quite without prospective or retroactive vindication of any kind.

Growing up in South Africa, as a child of immigrant Jewish parents, surrounded by many peoples in different stages of development, all of whom were still in fierce contention over their ultimate "title" to the land, I had as one group among my neighbors yet another chosen people: the Boers, or Afrikaners. Their national or collective myth about themselves owed almost everything to the Bible. Like the Israelites, and their fellow Calvinists in New England, they believed that they had been called by their God to wander through the wilderness, to meet and defeat the heathen, and to occupy a promised land on his behalf. How literally they took this parallel may be gauged from the fact that the holiest day of their national calendar bore the name "Day of the Covenant": this as an explicit reminder of the covenant established between the people of Israel and their God in the Sinai desert. (The Afrikaners' covenant commemorates the day when a party of Voortrekkers pledged themselves to the God of their fathers before going to do battle, successfully as it turned out, with the Zulus.) A sense of their having been summoned by divine decree to perform an ineluctable historical duty has never left the Boers, and has contributed to both their strength and their weakness.

But if one goes to the source of persistent, protean notions like these in a search for any kind of systematic elaboration of them, one is bound to be disappointed. I do not wish to extract a system of ideas from a text which does not contain one; or to impose such a system upon it. Rather, as I have said, I want to examine the moral drama which is to be found there: a drama which is acted out by "characters" who embody the deepest longings (and *hence* also the deepest fears) of its authors. Of these characters, the greatest is Yahweh himself: the God who chooses and rejects; who promises and denies; who fulfills all the yearnings of those who conceive him, and who punishes them for the very yearnings out of which they had created him. Through his actions and those of the others involved in the drama one can discern the perplexities and misgivings about the idea of a divine election which were felt by those with whom it had originated; one can make out also their attempts to resolve such difficulties. The God whom they had created filled them with pride and a sense of power. He also filled them with terror. Knowing more than they did about that creation, because we know all that has happened since, we can hardly feel these emotions to have been misplaced.

One final observation. The establishment of the modern state of Israel, and the ensuing wars between Arabs and Israelis, may give an appearance of strange topicality to some of what follows. It is not only as a Jew born and brought up in South Africa that I have felt the tensions of living in a land to which different peoples lay claim, by divine or quasi-divine right. It is also as one who always had a natural sympathy with the aims of the Zionist movement, and who has frequently spent longer or shorter spells of time in Israel.

History, T. S. Eliot said, has many cunning passages, contrived corridors. None has been so long, or has been traversed in such bloody circumstances, as that which has produced the modern state of Israel on the very site of the ancient Israel: the very site, therefore, of Canaan and Palestine. Ironically enough, during the two thousand years of their existence in the diaspora, the Jews generally avoided any kind of "politicization" of their claim to the Holy Land, let alone of their belief in their own chosenness. It was not until the advent of the modern era, and the growth of secularism, that political Zionism began to develop its appeal as a mass movement. Normative Judaism, the Judaism of the Talmud and the rabbis—which was the one great, internal force that had previously kept the Jews together—was in fact predicated on the continuance of their political powerlessness. It has often been said that the immense body of post-biblical teaching, law, and commentary, which it was the prime duty of a pious Jew to master and to live by, was in effect a portable substitute for the land and the sovereignty that had been lost. The restoration of these was believed by pious Jews to be wholly in the hands of their God. Needless to say, that did not save them from being accused of plotting to dominate the entire Christian world, whether through the poisoning of wells in the Middle Ages or through the manipulation of the stock exchange in modern times; but that is another matter.

From time to time, diaspora Jewry did succumb to fevers of messianic expectation, produced by various charlatans or megalomaniacs claiming to be the savior sent by heaven to redeem the people from captivity and dispersion. But the nature of such outbursts serves to show that the reestablishment of Jewish sovereignty in Palestine, as far as the mass of the Orthodox were concerned, was to take place "at the end of days," when history and society as they had been known would come to an end; it would be brought about through a divine act, as a reward for piety, never as the result of human scheming and ambition. This was how the prophets had seemed to speak of it, and in this respect the Orthodox were indeed their followers.

Hence the original response of Orthodox Jewry to the Zionist movement, and to its directly political aims and methods, was for the most part one of outright hostility;

there was even of horror at what was seen as a form of blasphemy. The Zionists, it was said, were "forcing the Messiah."

Now everything looks different. Israel has been reborn as a state, and today only the most extreme group among the Orthodox, inside and outside it, still refuse to recognize its existence. The rest have come to terms with what has been accomplished; and most have gone much further than that. Religious parties have their representatives in the Israeli parliament and cabinet; these representatives demand, often successfully, that the injunctions of Jewish (post-biblical) religious law be enforced by the authority of the state on believing and nonbelieving citizens alike. Moreover, many of them not only turn to the Bible to provide a justification for the establishment of the state, but cite various texts from it in order to "prove" that it is impermissible for any Israeli government to follow policies they dislike. This is true, for example, of those who would use particular verses from the books of Numbers and Joshua in order to forbid the partitioning in any way of the biblical land of Israel with the Arabs who live there.

It is in the very nature of the Jewish state that the Hebrew Scriptures will always be a source of pride and reassurance to its inhabitants, whether they are believers or not. To no other people does the Bible speak so intimately, or in such a directly inspiring fashion. Yet my view of the ultimate "message" of the biblical texts is rather different from that drawn by the zealots among them. It is amazing to think that the turmoils of our own time should in certain respects resemble some of the events described in the Scriptures. It is even more remarkable that these resemblances are in fact consequences of the story told there.

Orthodox Judaism and the Religion
of Israel: A Note

This book is for the most part focused on "the religion of Israel" as it is presented to us in the Scriptures, and *not* on rabbinic, or normative, Judaism, the religion practiced more or less devotedly by all observant Jews today. A few words to make clearer the distinction between the two might be helpful at this stage, rather than later.

Perhaps the simplest way of putting the matter is to say that the religion of Israel came into being in the six or seven hundred years between the Israelite conquest of Canaan (say 1200 B.C.) and the destruction of the Temple in Jerusalem by the Babylonians in 587 B.C.; Judaism, on the other hand, is derived from one strand of religious thought and practice which developed subsequently among the descendants of the Israelites, in Palestine, Babylon, and elsewhere. If the prime, indeed the only, source of information about the religion of Israel is the Scriptures, the primary document for the understanding of Judaism—alongside the Scriptures—is the Talmud, an immense compendium of law codes and commentaries extrapolated at ever-greater removes from the biblical legislation. The Talmud was put together over a period of something like the thousand years that followed upon the Babylonian conquest.

Now for some complications. The first is that rabbinic Judaism has always insisted that it is *identical* with the religion of Israel; and that every single one of the laws in the Talmud was actually given to Moses by Yahweh at Sinai, in the form of what is called the Oral Law, a kind of supplement to the Written Law to be found in the Scriptures. One need not give any credence to this claim in order to see that it is in itself an important fact about Judaism. In a somewhat analogous way, one need not accept the much less direct claim made by Christians that the "New Testament" is the fulfillment or completion of the "Old Testament" in order to take into account that claim when trying to understand Christianity.*

A second complication is that while it is true the Scriptures are our sole source of information about the pristine religion of Israel, they were put into the shape in which we have them not by the Israelites themselves, but by their descendants—those who were on the way to becoming Jews, as it were. The fall of Jerusalem in 587 B.C., and the exile to Babylon of leading groups of Israelites, serve as appropriately dramatic occasions to mark the beginning of the transition from the earlier form of the religion to the later. However, it is that very event—the destruction of Israelite nationhood, to put it starkly—which made the survivors eager to hasten the process of "fixing" and canonizing much of the great religious and historical inheritance that is the subject of this study. The issue of sovereignty over the land of Israel had always been at the very heart of the Israelite religion; now that that sovereignty was lost, the descendants of the Israelites, living either in exile or under a succession of foreign rulers (Persians, Greeks, Romans) in their homeland, made the religion turn increasingly upon the preservation and study of the documents which contained the records of the nation's independent existence: how it had been won, how it was lost, how it might be regained. Thus, in the words of the nineteenth-century German scholar Julius Wellhausen, under whose shadow most workers in the field still seem to labor, the Jews began transforming them-

---

* It is a striking but relatively little known fact that the core of the Talmud, the law code known as the Mishnah, appears to have been put into writing about a century *after* the last of the Gospels (John).

selves into "a religious community, *based upon the traditions of a national community that had ceased*"* (my ital-
ics).

In distinguishing between Judaism and the religion of
Israel, I am hardly trying to deny, therefore, the intimacy
of the relationship between them. It is not merely that the
later form of the religion claims to be dependent upon the
sanction of the Scriptures for all its own practices. There
is a sense in which it is also proper to say that the earlier
religion is dependent upon the later—it was the post-exilic
community which edited, collated, and added liberally to
the Scriptures, before the canon was finally closed in the
second century of the Christian era.

As far as this book is concerned, I shall assume that within
the Hebrew canon there are two identifiable bodies of writing: on the one hand, there are those writings—whether
of a narrative or prophetic or prescriptive nature—which
refer directly to the divine election of Israel, the revelation
of Yahweh to Moses, and the conquest and loss of the promised land; on the other hand, there is a related yet distinct
group of apocalyptic prophecies (parts of Daniel and Joel,
for example), as well as manuals of temple practice and a
group of wisdom writings, all of which are of later provenance. I am interested chiefly in the works in the former
category. I consider them as a whole, in the shape in which
they were left by the post-exilic collators and editors; I
do not try to look within them for those sections which
scholars would regard as "genuinely" of the period of which
they speak. One result of my concentration upon the overall
myth, incidentally, is that I virtually ignore many of the
biographical narratives, and entire books like Job or Eccle-

---

* *Prolegomena to the History of Israel.*

siastes, which have always been much favored by those who consider the Bible "as literature."

As for developments after the Babylonian exile which were eventually to lead to the emergence of rabbinic Judaism as well as of Christianity, I will mention here only three major historical events. The first of these must obviously be the permission given by Cyrus, king of Persia, to the exiles in Babylon to return to their homeland and rebuild their Temple. The second is the reestablishment by the Jews of their political independence under the Hasmonean kings, after the collapse of Greek rule, when it seemed (to some) that part of the glory of the Israelite past had at last been recaptured. The third is the Roman conquest of Jerusalem and the destruction of the Second Temple in A.D. 70. These were the circumstances that determined not merely the fortunes but the very forms of the different sects that regarded themselves as the true heirs of Israel. The strand in Judaism that was eventually to become normative, or Orthodox, is generally associated with just one of these sects—the Pharisees, who were the most zealous expounders and extenders of the Law; we know that there were others, like the Sadducees, who rejected the Oral Law entirely; as well as a variety of apocalyptic sects, who interpreted the Scriptures, the prophecies in particular, in the light of their own feverish expectations. Among these groups the earliest Christians must clearly be numbered.

CHAPTER ONE

LEAVING THE LAND

In the year 587 B.C. the armies of the Neo-Babylonian empire captured Jerusalem and destroyed the Temple of Yahweh. With that conquest, the story of the two Hebrew kingdoms which is told in different forms in the biblical books of Samuel, Kings, and Chronicles comes to its end.

Like most histories of public events, the tale told in these books, which cover a span of more than four hundred years, is ultimately a depressing one. It begins in warfare and ends with a war; it begins with civil dissension and ends with it; it begins and ends with acts of personal revenge and cruelty. In the course of the narrative we are told of the establishment by David of a kingdom which for the first time brought under a single administration all the tribes of Israel; of the succession to the throne of his son, Solomon; of the breakup, after Solomon's death, of the state into a northern kingdom (called, variously, Israel, Ephraim, or Samaria) and a southern kingdom, Judah; of the campaigns and patched-up treaties of peace between these two petty principalities; of their alliances and ruptures with neighboring states; of the ever-increasing pressure they came under from imperial powers like Egypt, Assyria, and Babylon, which were battling for possession of the land bridge between Asia and Africa.

The northern kingdom succumbed to Assyria in 722, and thereafter simply ceased to exist as a political entity. (Its people, too, virtually disappear from history at that point— and enter myth as the "Ten Lost Tribes.") The southern kingdom managed to survive a variety of assaults for another hundred and twenty-five years. In 597 B.C. the Babylonians (or "Chaldeans," as the chronicler sometimes refers to them) unseated King Jehoiachin, a descendant of the Davidic line, and carried him away as a captive to Babylon. In his place they put on the throne a young relation of the former king, Zedekiah by name, who was evidently expected to act as nothing more than their puppet.

This is the account given in 2 Kings of Zedekiah's reign, and of its end:

> Zedekiah was twenty-one years old when he became king, and he reigned eleven years in Jerusalem. His mother's name was Hamutal the daughter of Jeremiah of Libnah. And he did what was evil in the sight of the Lord, according to all that Jehoiakim had done. For because of the anger of the Lord it came to the point in Jerusalem and Judah that he cast them out from his presence.
>
> And Zedekiah rebelled against the king of Babylon. And in the ninth year of his reign, in the tenth month, on the tenth day of the month, Nebuchadnezzar king of Babylon came with all his army against Jerusalem, and laid siege to it; and they built siegeworks against it round about. So the city was besieged till the eleventh year of King Zedekiah. On the ninth day of the fourth month the famine was so severe in the city that there was no food for the people of the land. Then a breach was made in the city; the king with

all the men of war fled by night by the way of the gate between the two walls, by the king's garden, though the Chaldeans were around the city. And they went in the direction of the Arabah. But the army of the Chaldeans pursued the king, and overtook him in the plains of Jericho; and all his army was scattered from him. Then they captured the king, and brought him up to the king of Babylon at Riblah, who passed sentence upon him. They slew the sons of Zedekiah before his eyes, and put out the eyes of Zedekiah, and bound him in fetters, and took him to Babylon.

In the fifth month, on the seventh day of the month—which was the nineteenth year of King Nebuchadnezzar, king of Babylon—Nebuzaradan, the captain of the bodyguard, a servant of the king of Babylon, came to Jerusalem. And he burned the house of the Lord, and the king's house and all the houses of Jerusalem; every great house he burned down. And all the army of the Chaldeans, who were with the captain of the guard, broke down the walls around Jerusalem. And the rest of the people who were left in the city and the deserters who had deserted to the king of Babylon, together with the rest of the multitude, Nebuzaradan the captain of the guard carried into exile. But the captain of the guard left some of the poorest of the land to be vinedressers and ploughmen.

And the pillars of bronze that were in the house of the Lord, and the stands and the bronze sea that were in the house of the Lord, the Chaldeans broke in pieces, and carried the bronze to Babylon. And they took away the pots, and the shovels, and the snuffers, and the dishes for incense and all the vessels of bronze used in the temple service, the firepans also, and the bowls. What was of gold the captain of the guard took away as gold, and what was of silver, as silver. As for the two pillars, the one sea, and the stands, which Solomon had made for the house of the Lord, the bronze of all these vessels was beyond weight. The height of the one pillar was eighteen cubits, and upon it was a capital of bronze; the height of the capital was three cubits; a network and pomegranates, all of bronze, were upon the capital round about. And the second pillar had the like, with the network.

And the captain of the guard took Seraiah the chief priest, and Zephaniah the second priest, and the three keepers of the threshold; and from the city he took an officer who had been in command of the men of war, and five men of the king's council who were found in the city; and the secretary of the commander of the army who mustered the people of the land; and sixty men of the people of the land who were found in the city. And Nebuzaradan the captain of the guard took them, and brought them to the king of Babylon at Riblah. And the king of Babylon smote them, and put them to death at Riblah in the land of Hamath. So Judah was taken into exile out of its land.

24:18—25:21

Much of the power of the passage springs perhaps paradoxically from the bareness and matter-of-factness with which the story is told. In context, the account is more poignant than a single quotation can convey, for it comes at the end of chapter upon chapter devoted to descriptions of earlier threats and escapes, or partial escapes, by the kingdom and its people; of disasters which turn out to be, after all, not final; of accounts of other sieges and the piecemeal loss of the land; of catastrophes averted by chance or (in the eyes of the chronicler) by miracle. But this time there is no escape. No miracles intervene. No foreign power comes to the aid of the besieged populace. No mysterious plagues destroy the besieging army, as had once happened to the army of the Assyrians. In great detail, covering everything from the exact dates of particular events to their exact location, and with a careful avoidance of comment, the chronicler tells us just what happened, or was believed to have happened, and to whom; nothing more. It is enough. Across twenty-five centuries we recognize his sense of desolation and disbelief at what he has to record. Even the simplicity of mind he reveals in his account of the lost treasures of the Temple, and the provincial wonder he conveys at their workmanship and value, are highly expressive.

Simple, matter-of-fact, bare, provincial: these may be the appropriate words to describe the passage. Yet there are elements in it which are not simple at all. (Let me say again that I am not concerned with the historical veracity of the narrative. About that not even the apparent precision of the details can finally tell us very much.) For example, the God of Israel was believed by the biblical writers to participate actively and continuously in the history of his people, and the history of other peoples; we see him doing so here. The writers were convinced that his actions expressed his pleasure or displeasure with the behavior of his people and their leaders; those are the grounds given for his action here. The final punishment which Yahweh was believed to have meted out to his people for their disobedience was to take their land from them and send them into exile: that is what he does here. No distinction was made by the biblical writers between what we might think of as the domain of politics and the domain of religion, or even between the domain of error and the domain of sin; no such distinction is observed here.

The complexity of these issues, all of which will be examined later, is obvious enough. But it can at least be said of them here that they appear quite explicitly in the passage quoted. However, within that passage there are elements of equal importance, which are rather more difficult to discern.

Take, for instance, the account of the appalling revenge
taken on the Judean king and his family by the Babylonians.
The refinement of cruelty in compelling the deposed king
to watch the murder of his children just before he is blinded,
so that their death throes will be the last sight he will
ever look upon, may hardly seem to call for any special
comment. The episode appears to be nothing more than a
sickening barbarity of the kind that conquerors have perpe-
trated in all ages against people whom they have at their
mercy. Yet there is another, or additional, way of looking
at this particular item of information and the manner in
which it is presented. The sentence which actually describes
the punishment—"They slew the sons of Zedekiah before
his eyes, and put out the eyes of Zedekiah"—has a certain
punning quality, a seesaw quality, as it might be called,
which is much more than a surface effect. It reveals something deeply characteristic of the biblical writers' cast of
mind; a characteristic that can be seen both locally (as on
this occasion) and in the larger patterns of the prose narratives, as well as in the poetic writings of the prophets.

For instance, in the prophecies ascribed to a contemporary
of these very events, we read:

> As I live, says the Lord, though Coniah the son of
> Johoiakim, king of Judah, were the signet ring on my
> right hand, yet I would tear you off and give you into
> the hand of those who seek your life, into the hand
> of those of whom you are afraid, even into the hand
> of Nebuchadrezzar king of Babylon . . .
>   JEREMIAH 22:24–25

Or:

> And when your people say, 'Why has the Lord our
> God done all these things to us?' you shall say to them,
> 'As you have forsaken me and served foreign gods in

> your land, so you shall serve strangers in a land that
> is not yours.'
>
> JEREMIAH 5:19

Or:

> Therefore, thus says the Lord: You have not obeyed
> me by proclaiming liberty, every one to his brother
> and to his neighbour; behold, I proclaim to you liberty
> to the sword, to pestilence, and to famine, says the
> Lord.
>
> JEREMIAH 34:17

Or from words ascribed to an earlier prophet (but probably
written at a much later date, according to some scholars):

> Has he smitten them as he smote those who smote
>   them?
> Or have they been slain as their slayers were slain?
> Measure by measure, by exile thou didst contend with
>   them . . .
>
> ISAIAH 27:7-8

Such echoes and resemblances, which could be multiplied
many times over from the prophetic writers, may seem too
faint or random really to be meaningful. Yet in the extract
from 2 Kings given above we are actually told that Zedekiah,
whose blinding is so graphically presented to us, was a man
who had himself "done evil *in the sight of* the Lord." (So
had many of his predecessors on the throne, according to
the chronicler: the importance of the point in this context
will be made clear in a moment.) Moreover, in the original
Hebrew, the phrase translated as "in the sight of the Lord"
is, quite literally, *"in the eyes of the Lord"—be'einei Yahweh.* Thus—and I advise the reader to take the next few
phrases slowly—the man who did evil in the eyes of the
Lord suffers the punishment of having his own eyes put

out; but only after they have witnessed the sight he would most have wished to be spared. Furthermore, through the murder of his children, the fact that he is to be the very last, the end-point, of a long line of such wrongdoing kings is presented dramatically to him, so to speak, as well as to us, the readers of the tale.

It will become clear in the pages that follow why I consider this kind of patterning of events, and indeed of words, so important. For the moment I will merely say that even in this case, in what appears to be a purely "objective" account of a physical action, we have an illustration or expression of that sense of a remorseless *reciprocity* governing the processes of history which seems central to the biblical writers' moral and imaginative life, and hence to the way in which they perceived the world. To avoid misunderstanding, I should add that the concept of reciprocity, as it will be developed in these pages, goes far beyond the idea of a simple application of the *lex talionis*—"life for life, eye for eye, tooth for tooth"—which most people might be inclined to think of immediately in connection with Zedekiah's fate; it would include but also go beyond the special covenant or mutually binding contract between God and people which is so striking a feature of the Israelite religion. What I have in mind is not a conviction or a belief, but rather something lying so deep within the writers' minds it ultimately determines the possibilities of conviction and belief.

Every act or condition, in this view, contains within it, and will sooner or later generate, its opposite; every deed and every claim will produce another that will balance it, or invert it, or reverse it—and will do so with such exactitude that distinctions between words like "opposition" and "complement" become blurred and irrelevant, as if in some primitively Hegelian universe. Inversions and ironies of this kind are essential to the nature of the deity, as the writers seem to have conceived it; indeed, one might claim that it is his activation of such inversions and ironies, his sleepless awareness of them, his containment of them within himself, with all their unexpected consequences, that show him to be truly and irresistibly divine. Hence the endless to-and-fro or seesaw motion between reward and punishment, between blessing and curse, between gift and retraction, between choice and rejection, through which the story dramatizes the relations between the deity and his people. As the prophet Jeremiah puts it (51:56), holding the balance finely between the positive and negative senses of repayment: "The Lord is a God of recompense; he will surely requite."

It has often been said that Yahweh's catastrophic intervention in the history of his people produces, with the fall of Jerusalem, an astonishing inversion of what might seem to be the "normal" response to a national disaster. Why is the defeat of the people of Israel, which the passage records with so much intensity, not also a defeat for their God? Because it has been transformed into a victory for him! In the first place, the defeat of Judah is a demonstration of *his* power: it is by his will, not that of the Babylonian rulers and captains, that the city is conquered and his own Temple desecrated. In the second place, it is a demonstration of his moral consistency. Having warned the people of Israel what the consequences of their sins would be, he is as good as his word, and shows his anger by driving his disobedient people out of their country. So much for the explicit "lessons" drawn from the event. To these I would add another, which I shall illustrate in the next chapter. The punishment of exile matches and balances exactly not just the favor he had originally done for his own people, but also, and quite as importantly, the disfavor he had previously shown to the enemies of Israel. Thus he reveals the laws of reciprocity which express his nature.

Those are the consolations which the chronicler manages to secure from the national humiliation he has to record. They are purely verbal, imaginative, retrospective consolations, no doubt; fantasy consolations, if you wish. But they were not the less fateful, for Jews, Christians, and everyone else, for being so. Once the Israelites were persuaded by the biblical writers to accept the moral responsibility for their exile and enslavement, it became necessary for them to see suffering and dispossession, weakness and shame, as being as much the marks of God's favor as success and victory had been. This could be achieved by projecting the laws of reciprocity forward into a history still to be unfolded.

CHAPTER TWO

THE CONQUEST OF THE LAND

In driving his people out of their land, the God of Israel was doing to them exactly what he had done to others, centuries before, on their behalf. For the story of the king-doms told in the books of Samuel, Kings, and Chronicles is preceded by that told in the books of Numbers, Joshua, and Judges, which gives an account of the Israelite conquest of the land; just as that story, in turn, is preceded (in terms of the "plot," if not necessarily or entirely in order of being committed to writing) by the first four books of the Scrip-tures, which set out the express conditions upon which God is said to have given the land to his people.

From the very first mention of that land, however, it is made clear that the place set aside for the Israelites is not an empty or untenanted one. It has its own people, who consider it to be theirs. Or, as Genesis succinctly puts it:

> At that time the Canaanites were in the land. Then the Lord appeared to Abram, and said, 'To your descen-dants I will give this land.' So he built there an altar to the Lord, who had appeared to him.
>
> 12:6–7

And a few chapters further on, when the promise that God makes to Abraham is repeated, the land is defined even more elaborately and grandiosely, both geographically and by the names of the peoples who live there.

> On that day the Lord made a covenant with Abram, saying, 'To your descendants I give this land, from the river of Egypt to the great river, the river Euphrates, the land of the Kenites, the Kenizzites, the Kadmonites, the Hittites, the Perizzites, the Rephaim, the Amorites, the Canaanites, the Girgashites and the Jebusites.'
>
> 15:18–21

What is to be done with these peoples, or at any rate the more accessible of them, when the descendants of Abraham return to Canaan, after the many generations of their sojourn in Egypt?

> I will send my terror before you, and will throw into confusion all the people against whom you shall come, and I will make all your enemies turn their backs to you. And I will send hornets before you, which shall drive out Hivite, Canaanite, and Hittite from before you. I will not drive them out from before you in one year, lest the land become desolate and the wild beasts multiply against you. Little by little I will drive them out from before you, until you are increased and possess the land. And I will set your bounds from the Red Sea to the sea of the Philistines, and from the wilderness to the Euphrates; for I will deliver the inhabitants of the land into your hand, and you shall drive them out before you.
>
> Exodus 23:27–31

But as the very last words of that passage make clear, God does not undertake to do all the work single-handed; he will play his part in clearing the land only if the Israelites do their share—and what their share is to be is made absolutely explicit in many passages. Whether the Israelite occupation of the land of Canaan was a relatively bloodless affair, as some historians appear to believe, or a series of purposeful and savage campaigns in which large parts of the countryside were taken over and their inhabitants wiped out, as others contend, does not matter here. What the biblical writers wanted to believe, and wanted everyone else to believe, is plain enough. A *herem* was placed upon the peoples of Canaan: a ban, a curse, in terms of which they were devoted to destruction. "Men, women, and children" were to be put to the sword or driven out; they, their religion, and (not least) their women were a source of pollution; to show mercy to them was a sin and an offense to the God of Israel; to leave them in possession of any part of the country was to lay up a store of trouble for the future, for they would inevitably lure the Israelites away from the worship of the true God.

Of course, the more vehemently this last point is insisted upon, the more clearly we can see how tempting the Canaanite civilization and its corruptions must have seemed to the invading people.

> You shall tear down their altars, and break their pillars, and cut down their Asherim (for you shall worship no other god, for the Lord, whose name is Jealous, is a jealous God), lest you make a covenant with the inhabitants of the land, and when they play the harlot after their gods and sacrifice to their gods and one invites you, you eat of his sacrifice, and you take of their daughters for your sons, and their daughters play the harlot after their gods and make your sons play the harlot after their gods.
>
> EXODUS 34:13–16

All this hatred and fear, all the exterminatory zeal which is expressed in many passages (whether or not these accurately reflect the facts of the occupation), actually make it all the more remarkable that the writers should also have been so emphatic about the fate of the Canaanites paralleling or foreshadowing exactly that of their own people. The "bloodthirsty fantasies" (as the accounts of the occupation have been described by one writer) which appear in the books dealing with the conquest are often quoted to illustrate the primitive nature of the morality to be found in the earlier Hebrew Scriptures, especially when it is compared with the moral teachings which appear in the writings of the prophets, let alone with those in the Gospels. To read the text as a whole, however, is to find that while the "early" morality of the Scriptures is primitive indeed, that does not necessarily mean it is simple. Equally, one may find that the much-praised loftiness of spirit which manifests itself in the prophetic books, and in the New Testament, has plenty in it that is archaic and bloodthirsty enough.

Anyway, at no point does one find an explicit expression of misgiving or compunction on the part of the writers about the fate of the Canaanites. Whatever else might be said about the ancient Israelites, therefore, they cannot be accused of suffering from the pangs of a guilty conscience as a result of their conquest of the land and the dispossession of its native inhabitants. No fashionable, contemporary "liberal guilt" for them! Or so it may seem. Yet an unmistakable note of moral unease, to put it no more strongly than that for the moment, is surely evident in those passages which try to present some kind of justification on God's behalf for what was done to the people of the country. Deuteronomy 9:4 tells us that he drove them out because of their "wickedness"; Leviticus 18:24–26, 28, referring to child sacrifice, and to sexual transgressions of various kinds (incest, homosexuality, relations with a menstruating woman), makes the point at greater length:

> Do not defile yourselves by any of these things, for by all these the nations I am casting out before you defiled themselves; and the land became defiled, so that I punished its iniquity, and the land vomited out its inhabitants. But you shall keep my statutes and my ordinances and do none of these abominations, either the native or the stranger who sojourns among you . . . lest the land vomit you out, when you defile it, as it vomited out the nation that was before you.

Since there is no record in the Scriptures of God's having made the particular "statutes and ordinances" referred to in that book known to the Canaanites—and indeed, it is quite specifically stated that his revelation of them to the Israelites was a wholly unprecedented event—this justification of the savage treatment urged against the "men of the land" is a rather unconvincing one.* However, there can be no gainsaying the force of the threat in the last verse of this passage. It is *there*, in the notion of what can be called a reciprocal or tit-for-tat expulsion, that we can discern the real "moral" of the story of the relationship between God, the Israelites, and the Canaanites. It is a moral the writers were only partially conscious of, as the rationalization of their God's motivation for his treatment of the natives suggests; but one which they nevertheless managed to suggest.

---

* Some would argue that a notion of a self-evident or reasonable moral code in the relationships between men is more or less assumed throughout the Scriptures; and that this is what the Canaanites can therefore be supposed to have transgressed. My own view is that to argue in these terms is to go against the overpowering emphasis the text places everywhere on God's direct *commandment* as the sole source of every kind of law. (See Chapter Four.)

"Never trust the teller; trust the tale." D. H. Lawrence's dictum is probably the single most famous sentence in English literary criticism. If we apply it here, we see that the "tale" is plain enough; in fact, it could hardly be plainer. At the behest of their God, a people comes out of the desert into the land described as that of the Amorites, the Canaanites, and the rest: "a land flowing with milk and honey . . . a land of hills and valleys, which drinks water by the rain from heaven . . . a land of wheat and barley, of vines and fig trees and pomegranates." God gives the newcomers the right, or rather imposes upon them the obligation, to do away with the peoples who are already there: they are "utterly [to] destroy them . . . and show no mercy to them." Centuries pass, and the conquerors are in turn dispossessed by cruel invaders, acting on behalf of that same God, and are driven into exile: thus suffering exactly the same fate that the despised and hated aboriginals had once suffered. That is the essential outline of the tale which has been handed down to us.

Only . . . The people who came out of the desert to conquer the land of Canaan had themselves been enslaved in a previous phase of the story; in their subsequent exile they looked forward passionately to the state they had previously known. In that series of events, in such protracted but ineluctable reversals of historical fortune, the writers of the story seemed to believe their God had shown himself. That was how he made his world work. That was how he revealed the nature of his moral being.

Look back now to the passage quoted from 2 Kings in the previous chapter. There the writers succeeded in making a victory (of a kind) out of their terrible defeat at the hands of the Babylonians. Here they can be seen making a defeat (of a kind) out of their conquest of the Canaanites. "I will do to you," God says in Leviticus 33:56, "as I thought to do to them." And in Deuteronomy 8:20, "Like the nations that the Lord makes to perish before you, so shall you perish."

At this point readers who know the Bible might want to protest at the way I have told the "tale." *Of course,* they would say, the possibility or even the likelihood of the Israelites' losing the land was implicit in their taking possession of it; or rather it was not implicit at all, as my own quotations make clear, but absolutely explicit. The conditions on which Yahweh made the land over to the Israelites could hardly be presented more directly or more forcefully than they are. The Israelites are Yahweh's chosen people: chosen to receive both his Law and the Land. But it is made clear to them that they cannot have the latter without the former. If they cease to obey the Law, they will lose the Land—as eventually they do. That and nothing else is the moral of the story.

> When you beget children and children's children, and have grown old in the land, if you act corruptly by making a graven image in the form of anything, and by doing what is evil in the sight of the Lord your God, so as to provoke him to anger, I call heaven and earth to witness against you this day, that you will soon utterly perish from the land which you are going over the Jordan to possess; you will not live long upon it, but will be utterly destroyed. And the Lord will scatter you among the peoples, and you will be left few in number among the nations where the Lord will drive you.
>
> DEUTERONOMY 4:25–27

In replying to this objection I shall make one relatively minor point, and then another which does not seem to me minor at all. In terms of the "plot," it is significant that those Canaanites who remain in the land are always spoken of as a snare and temptation; by leading the Israelites astray they will bring them into the disfavor of their God, with all the dire consequences that must flow therefrom. And that is eventually what is said to happen. Thus the Canaanites are not simply got out of the way, but do continue to play a role in the drama and to affect the course of events; crucially so, in the end. The Israelites conquer the Canaanites; then they are conquered (in another sense of the word) by the Canaanite gods; in consequence the Israelites, too, are expelled from the land. In terms of the story we are told, should we see this as a form of revenge by the Canaanites for what had been done to them? Perhaps that will seem fanciful to some readers.* However, there is a much larger issue involved here. What is at stake is the question of how seriously one is prepared to take Yahweh's status as a fiction.

To say that the only moral which the tale enforces is that the Israelites were driven out of the land because of their disobedience to the commands of God is to do no more than repeat what the Bible tells us. But that must be the starting point of any secular interpretation of the Scriptures, not its terminus. As far as I am concerned, the story to be investigated *is* precisely what others would call its "moral": by which I mean the actions of a God who singles out peoples for special favors and punishments, together with the reasons proffered by the narrators for his so doing. I am not disputing the historicity of certain central

---

* It is significant that the Philistines, who appear to have been at first a much greater threat, militarily speaking, to the consolidation of the Israelite hold on Judea and Samaria, virtually drop out of the story after the conquest. Since their lands were not occupied, they presented no threat to the inner or spiritual well-being of the historians and prophets of Israel.

events alluded to in the text. But if you do not believe in the objective existence of Yahweh, or of any being resembling him, you have to see the entire record, of which his pronouncements and the actions imputed to him are only a part, as the precipitate of conflicting human memories, desires, wish fulfillments, anxieties, and so forth; all these having been shaped by, and then attempting to give shape to, particular and often desperate historical exigencies.

To do this does not compel you to adopt a simple-mindedly "Marxist" view of the text overall. Of course, the religion can be interpreted as the articulation of an "ideology" appropriate to the situation in which the original Israelites found themselves. Yahweh enters their story, with his revelation of himself by name to Moses, just when they were about to become engaged in a life-and-death struggle to drive another people out of a land which they wanted to occupy and enjoy. What could be more convenient for the newcomers to believe than that they had been specially chosen, by divine decree, to perform the task of cleansing the land of its inhabitants? Why should they not subscribe to a set of beliefs and rituals which would mark them off as sharply as possible from those with whom they were at war?

But unlike an ideology, an unfolding story or dramatic myth has an inner dynamic which springs precisely from that which would be a weakness in the other form of discourse—its ambiguity. It has a habit, as it were, of saying more than one thing at a time, and more than those who create it and those who attend to it actually want to hear. In seeking to explain the past and control the future, the myth is compelled to remember that which it seeks to suppress, as well as that which it publicly celebrates; it has to present as living possibilities, sometimes even as attractive possibilities, alternative ways of acting and thinking to those it supposedly wishes to endorse. Hence the conflicts which are at its heart; hence the pleasure we feel in imaginatively living through them; hence, also, the possibility of the myth or story itself generating unexpected or unacknowledged misgivings through its very attempt to exorcise others.

With all this in mind, it does not seem to be at all gratuitous to regard the repeated harking back by the biblical writers to the fate of the Canaanites—both as a cause for thankfulness and as a terrible warning to themselves—as the expression of a deep-seated historical and moral tension or anxiety within the Israelite folk memory. Indeed, I do not know how else we can look upon it. This view can only be strengthened, moreover, by the scholarly argument that the invocations in Deuteronomy and Leviticus of the penalty of exile, as a punishment for following the ways of the Canaanites, are *post facto:* that is, written when either the fact or at least the possibility of subjugation and exile confronted the Israelites. After hundreds of years of possession of the land, how did the writers describe the nature of the punishment that was being meted out to their own people? What was the analogy that sprang at once to their minds?

More will be said later on these topics. In the meantime, as an illustration of how the story should be read as a whole if its moral burden is to be understood, I would like to take up the treatment of one recurring image, or cluster of images, which is absolutely central to any drama of conquest and dispossession. The texts in question speak of the material goods—the houses, the crops, the artifacts—which in all territorial wars pass from the losers directly into the hands of the victors.

38   THE STORY OF THE STORIES

> And when the Lord your God brings you into the land
> which he swore to your fathers, to Abraham, to Isaac,
> and to Jacob, to give you, with great and goodly cities,
> which you did not build, and houses full of all good
> things, which you did not fill, and cisterns hewn out,
> which you did not hew, and vineyards and olive trees,
> which you did not plant, and when you eat and are
> full, then take heed lest you forget the Lord, who
> brought you out of the land of Egypt, out of the house
> of bondage.
>
> DEUTERONOMY 6:10–12

The note of warning which is struck in the last sentence, and which is developed in the following verse of that chapter, can hardly be said to modify the belief this passage attempts to convey: that the God of Israel has done his people a great favor in allowing them to seize and enjoy the use of the possessions of others. Indeed, the warning only serves to emphasize just how wonderful is the favor he has done to them: be sure, it in effect says, that you feel a proper degree of gratitude for the good turn you have received. The celebratory intensity of the passage no doubt owes something to the historical memory of a poverty-stricken nomad or seminomad people responding to the ac-cumulated wealth of a developed, settled agricultural and urban community; but the unconscious pathos this might suggest hardly makes the sentiment expressed a more attrac-tive one. "Do not fear the people of the land," says Caleb (Numbers 14:9) with great succinctness and vividness, "for they are bread for us"—a declaration which promptly wins him the direct approval of his God.

Morally speaking, such utterances are at one with the ethos of all those verses which call for the wholesale destruc-tion of the Canaanites, and which specify that only on the pain of their suffering God's displeasure can any of them be spared. One cannot help comparing the delight which is repeatedly expressed in the seizing of the Canaanites' goods with the revealing concession made in the book of Deuteronomy to certain categories of men among the Israelites who are called up for service in war.

> Then the officers shall speak to the people, saying, 'What man is there that has built a new house and has not dedicated it? Let him go back to his house, lest he die in the battle and another man dedicate it. And what man is there that has planted a vineyard and has not enjoyed its fruit? Let him go back to his house, lest he die in the battle and another man enjoy its fruit. And what man is there that has betrothed a wife and has not taken her? Let him go back to his house, lest he die in the battle and another man take her.'
>
> 20:5–7

So *that* is how strongly the Israelites felt about the right of a man to enjoy the fruit of his labor! How then, one asks, could they not juxtapose that ruling with the pleasure taken in the thought of the despoliation of the Canaanites?

Well, they did. In a sense, that is the point I am making. Both passages are there, in the text of Deuteronomy, not very far from one another. Admittedly, on one level the meaning of the juxtaposition is simple and familiar enough to every one of us. If this or that misfortune happens to our enemies, and we benefit from it, then it's a very good thing; if, on the other hand, it happens to *us*, or even to just some of us, then it's very bad. On other levels, though, more complicated things are taking place in Deuteronomy, and beyond it; were this not true, the Hebrew Scriptures would ultimately have meant no more to the world than, say, all those Assyrian and Babylonian dispatches recording in exultantly gruesome detail the victories of one or another forgotten king over one or another enslaved and forgotten people.

For example, the good fortune which the divinity has graciously granted to his people, in bestowing on them the possessions of the Canaanites, is precisely inverted, as a prospect at least, by the time we come to the great series of blessings and curses which form the dramatic climax of Deuteronomy.

> You shall betroth a wife, and another man shall lie with her; you shall build a house, and you shall not dwell in it; you shall plant a vineyard, and you shall not use the fruit of it.
>
> 28:30

These images—the house and the vineyard wrested from the ownership of one people and given to another—are persistently invoked in other narrative and prophetic books: Joshua (24:13), Jeremiah (6:16), Isaiah (62:8), Amos (5:11), Micah (6:15), the Psalms (105:44), Nehemiah (9:25).* Invoked, that is, as a doom hanging over Israel as well as an example of God's kindness to the people in the past.

Moreover, among the last prophecies assigned to Amos and the Second Isaiah there are some verses differing only very slightly from one another in the two books, which seem to be an attempt to imagine an end to that pitiless sequence or alternation whereby the gain of the people of Israel has to be the loss of another, and vice versa, through all eternity. Speaking of Yahweh's plan for the return of Israel from exile ("I will shake the house of Israel among all the nations as one shakes with a sieve, but no pebble shall fall upon the earth"), the version in the book of Amos concludes:

---

* The list is not by any means exhaustive.

'I will restore the fortunes of my people Israel,
    and they shall rebuild the ruined cities and inhabit
       them;
they shall plant vineyards and drink their wine,
    and they shall make gardens and eat their fruit.
I will plant them upon their land,
    and they shall never again be plucked up
    out of the land which I have given them,'
                    says the Lord your God.

                        9:14–15

Notice: *they*, not another people unwittingly working on their behalf, shall rebuild the cities they inhabit; *they* shall plant the vineyards whose wine they drink. Then they shall never again be plucked up.

CHAPTER THREE

THE CHOICE

Continuing to work backward, as it were, we come to a question which is logically anterior to the issues raised by the Israelites' conquest of Canaan; indeed, it is anterior to almost everything in the Scriptures. Why did Yahweh choose the children of Israel to be "his own possession among the peoples"?

The short answer to this question is that he chose them because they wanted to believe that they had been chosen. They invented him, one can say, *so that* they might be chosen. They wanted to be exalted above other nations— "high above . . . in praise and in fame and in honour" (Deuteronomy 26:19)—and they ascribed precisely that ambition on their behalf to the most exalted being it was possible for them to conceive. From their belief in the intentions he nourished on their behalf, they derived a sense of inner strength and cohesion which they could not have got from any other source: a conviction of their own superiority over all the nations who had not been chosen.

All that, in terms of the general argument, may seem obvious enough. Motives and sentiments of the kind just described emerge clearly from the famous hymn of praise to Yahweh in Exodus, which celebrates not only the destruction of the Egyptian army that had been pursuing the fleeing Israelites, but also the forthcoming destruction of their enemies-to-be in the land of Canaan.

> Who is like thee, O Lord, among the gods?
> Who is like thee, majestic in holiness,
> terrible in glorious deeds, doing wonders?
> Thou didst stretch out thy right hand,
> the earth swallowed them.
> Thou hast led in thy steadfast love the people whom
>   thou hast redeemed,
> thou hast guided them by thy strength to thy holy abode.
> The peoples have heard, they tremble;
> pangs have seized on the inhabitants of Philistia.
> Now are the chiefs of Edom dismayed;
> the leaders of Moab, trembling seizes them;
> all the inhabitants of Canaan have melted away.
> Terror and dread fall upon them; because of the great
>   ness of thy arm, they are as still as a stone,
> till thy people, O Lord, pass by,
> till the people pass by whom thou hast purchased.
> Thou wilt bring them in, and plant them on thy own
>   mountain,
> the place, O Lord, which thou hast made for thy abode,
> the sanctuary, O Lord, which thy hands have estab
>   lished.
>
> 15:11–17

The claim to the territory made in that hymn has two aspects, one of them more encouraging to the Israelites than the other. On the one hand, it says that their title to the land resides in the fact that it has been given to them by a being supreme even "among the gods"; no one can have prior or more important rights to it than themselves, because no one has authority over God; certainly not the land's original inhabitants and its neighbors, who are mentioned one by one merely in order to be disposed of. (For the time being, at least.) Furthermore, God is expressly said to have chosen the land not only for the Israelites but also for himself: it is his own mountain, his abode, and the place where he has established his sanctuary. On the other hand, the very fact that he is praised and thanked for giving the land to the people, and that praising and thanking him for this reason is to be a central feature of his cult,* once they have been brought in and his sanctuary has been established, serve as a constant reminder to them that their possession of the land is not and never has been something "natural," or self-evident, or to be taken for granted. It is the result of a special intervention on their behalf by God into the processes of history; by its very nature such an intervention can be undone or can take a different form on another occasion, should the need arise. One such occasion, when he intervened to the harm of the Israelites, has already been looked at. So have some of the consequences of the self-consciousness which the Israelites had about their relationship to the territory they inhabited. Others still wait to be examined.

In any event, we have moved almost imperceptibly from discussing the apparently unlimited power of an unlimited divinity to something much more modest in scope. After all, what has the power ascribed to Yahweh in that paean of praise from Exodus actually produced? What has he delivered? A measured answer is to be found in Spinoza's *A Theologico-Political Treatise:*

Next I inquired, why the Hebrews were called God's chosen people, and discover[ed] that it was only because God has chosen

---

* The words "cult" and "cultic" are used throughout in their traditional sense: "in reference to external rites and ceremonies" *(Shorter Oxford English Dictionary).* That is, the words relate specifically and directly to the formal, public modes of worship adopted by the community of believers.

them for a certain strip of territory, where they might live peace-
ably and at ease. I learnt that the Law revealed by God to Moses
was merely the law of the independent Hebrew state. . . .

Their choice and vocation consisted only in temporal happiness
and the advantages of independent rule. . . . In the law no other
reward is offered for obedience other than the continual happiness
of an independent commonwealth and other goods of this life.

Spinoza comes to this conclusion only after considering
and recoiling from another possibility; the very notion of
chosenness with which I opened this chapter:

> Every man's true happiness and blessedness consist solely in
> the enjoyment of what is good, not in the pride that he alone
> is enjoying it, to the exclusion of others. He who thinks himself
> the more blessed because he is enjoying benefits which others
> are not, or because he is more blessed or more fortunate than
> his fellows, is ignorant of true happiness and blessedness, and
> the joy which he feels is either childish or envious and
> malicious. For instance, a man's true happiness consists only
> in wisdom, and the knowledge of the truth, not at all in the
> fact that he is wiser than others, or that others lack such
> knowledge. . . .
>
> When Scripture, therefore, in exhorting the Hebrews to obey
> the law, says that the Lord has chosen them for Himself before
> other nations (Deuteronomy 10:15); that He is near them, but
> not near others (Deuteronomy 4:7); that to them alone He has
> given just laws (Deuteronomy 4:8); and lastly, that He has marked
> them out before others (Deuteronomy 4:32); it speaks only ac-
> cording to the understanding of its hearers, who . . . knew not
> true blessedness. For in good sooth they would have been no
> less blessed if God had called all men equally to salvation, nor
> would God have been less present to them for being equally pres-
> ent to others; their laws would have been no less just if they
> had been ordained for all, and they themselves would have been
> no less wise.

What Spinoza has done here is simply to exclude from serious consideration those passages in the biblical text which offend him. That is the effect of his saying that such passages were put there merely to appeal to "the understanding of its hearers." The only evidence he can produce for this remark is his own humane but unfalteringly rational estimation of where and how "true happiness and blessedness" are to be found. The fact is, however, that the verses he cites from Deuteronomy speak of Israel's special privileges before Yahweh with exactly the same degree of sincerity and fervor as they do of everything else they touch upon; and we can safely assume that those who composed them were as liberally endowed with the particular kinds of childishness, enviousness, and malice which Spinoza deplores as their "hearers" were. Or as we are today.

Where the biblical writers differ from the rest of us (as Spinoza himself puts it in another context) is in their "unusually vivid imaginations." They revealed their imaginative power, I would argue, quite as much in the running account they give us of the relations between God and his chosen people as in the individual visions and tales which the larger narrative contains. Like every highly developed work of the imagination, the biblical "story of the stories" has the effect of showing us just how inextricably intertwined, in the depths of the psyche, are the connections between our benevolent and malevolent impulses, between childishness and maturity, between envy and generosity. As dramatists or storytellers (though not as philosophers), the biblical writers knew more about themselves and the rest of us than Spinoza gave them credit for; they certainly knew more than he did about the perils as well as the advantages of the special relationship they claimed to have with their God.

Thus, while exulting over Yahweh's choice, and rejoicing in the discomfiture of their enemies, who had been passed over and rejected, the composers of the biblical story could never lose sight of the terrifying possibility that it might be their turn next to join the ranks of the rejected. That was the danger to which they had exposed themselves imaginatively in evoking a God who exercised choices of such a fateful kind; that was the price they had to pay for the favor he had bestowed upon them. The constant presence of the possibility of such a rejection is one of the wonders of the entire tale. Sooner or later it is bound to happen, the story implicitly tells us, to those who seek preferment or special terms from the world all men are compelled to live in. Which is not to say, the story also tells us, that they will ever desist from seeking such preferment, and trying their hardest to get away with it unscathed. The explicit moral is that the people of Israel fall into God's disfavor only when they disobey him; the tacit moral is that *the very notion of having been chosen by such a God will produce the retribution appropriate to it.* It is, I suspect, because the former moral is urged upon us with such exhaustive vehemence that the latter has been virtually overlooked.

Anyway, if one returns to the opening question, and rephrases it to ask why, in the estimation of the Israelites themselves, Yahweh *had* chosen them to be his special possession among the nations, one sees that it calls for answers of two different kinds. Firstly, it can be answered in terms of the religious and historical purposes God is supposed to have had in mind in making such a choice. Secondly, one can try to explain why this particular people rather than some other was chosen to fulfill those special purposes.

Now, while the Scriptures have a great deal to say about the first kind of explanation—that is, about Yahweh's intentions for his chosen—they tell us practically nothing, explicitly at least, about his reasons for making *this* choice "from all other people that are upon the face of the earth" (Exodus 33:15). This is not because the writers took Yahweh's choice wholly for granted, or assumed that the reasons for it would be self-evident. Far from it. Indeed, the sense of being forever *on trial,* which is one of the consequences of the apparent arbitrariness of the claim to have been specially chosen, is a constant in Israelite and Jewish history.

The formal explanations as to why the choice fell on the Israelites rather than on some other people always refer back to previous commitments by Yahweh—which are themselves then left entirely unexplained. In Exodus we are told that God intends to redeem the people from slavery in Egypt because he has "remembered" the covenant he made with the patriarchs; in Deuteronomy this is forcefully repeated several times. In Deuteronomy also the Israelites are explicitly told that it was *not* because of their "righteousness" or "uprightness" that they were chosen by Yahweh, or because they were powerful or many in number; in Exodus God actually makes the suggestion to Moses (a suggestion which is elaborately recalled in Numbers 14 and Deuteronomy 9) that he should simply abandon or destroy the Israelites in the desert. Then he and Moses might begin all over again with another, less contumacious people, who would be more obedient to the Law and hence truly deserving of the promised land.

The intention of all these rebukes and warnings is obviously to make the people of Israel feel thoroughly humble about the favor that Yahweh has done them. The effect, however, is to make his choice seem more random and hence more unfathomable and more alarming than ever. This impression can only be strengthened when we turn to the promises in Genesis which are so insistently referred to as the ultimate source of all Yahweh's commitments to the children of Israel.* Why does God declare to Abraham that *he* should go from his country and his kindred and his father's house to the land that would be shown to him, where he would become "a great nation"? We are not told. Why, among Abraham's sons, does God choose Isaac to be the one with whom he will establish an "everlasting covenant," while proffering to Ishmael the consolation of fathering another, uncovenanted nation? We are not told. Why is Jacob preferred above his brother Esau; or to put the story in another way, why is Jacob allowed to cheat Esau out of his father's blessing, so that the divine prophecy made to Rebecca ("two people born of you shall be divided;

---

* For reasons already given, the argument is not really affected by the fact that some or even all of these promises may have been retrospectively written into earlier legends which were originally without them. To say of something which appears in an otherwise "early" text that it is a relatively late interpolation does not disqualify it from being treated, in my terms, as an integral part of the story. Exactly the opposite is true. Such "backing and filling," of which there is clearly a great deal, shows how keenly the writers and editors of the text felt the need to harmonize the tales they already had, from whatever sources they came, with any additional material they wished to incorporate into the story. In other words, they tried, at least intermittently, to view the text as a whole, and wanted it *to be viewed* as a whole.

A particularly obvious, and in my opinion particularly moving, example of the use made by the writers of the opportunities given to them for a retrospective enlargement and self-endorsement of the legends of the patriarchs is to be found in Genesis 15:12–15, which "looks forward" vividly to what is already known, in terms of the myth, to have taken place:

> As the sun was going down, a deep sleep fell on Abram; and lo, a dread and great darkness fell upon him. Then the Lord said to Abram, 'Know of a surety that your descendants will be sojourners in a land that is not theirs, and will be slaves there, and they will be oppressed for four hundred years; but I will bring judgment on the nation which they serve, and afterward they shall come out with great possessions. As for yourself, you shall go to your fathers in peace; you shall be buried in a good old age. . . .'

the one shall be stronger than the other") might be fulfilled in Jacob's favor? Again, we are not told. Abraham and one particular line descending from him are chosen: that is all. An anthropologist may declare, as Edmund Leach does in *Genesis as Myth and Other Essays*, that the reason for the choice is essentially that this line is the "purest" in blood, since Sarah, Isaac's mother, is Abraham's half-sister, which the mother of Ishmael is not; but from our point of view that merely puts the question back a stage further. We still have to ask: Why *this* line? The "purity" of the line from Abraham and his family matters, after all, only because he has already been chosen. As for Jacob and Esau, who are not merely born of the same mother but are twins, the one is preferred above the other when they are still in the womb: "the elder shall serve the younger." (A reversal of the primogenitive order is found in many biblical narratives; the case of David, which is mentioned below, is one of the most striking of these.) It cannot be said that the patriarchs are chosen for their special virtues; if anything, the case is exactly the other way around: whatever virtues are ascribed to them appear to spring from the fact that they have been specially favored or elected—and that they know it.

Now, one might argue—as Thomas Mann does in *Joseph and His Brothers*, a series of ironic, avowedly fictional variations upon the legends of Genesis—that in this respect Yahweh's actions are very much like those of life itself, which also "chooses" with apparent capriciousness those people whom it blesses (and curses) with gifts of any kind, and which invariably lets them know that they have been so chosen. (In 1 Samuel 16, to take an example from much later in the story, David is described as a handsome youth, with particularly beautiful eyes; but the "Spirit of the Lord" comes "mightily upon him" only *after* Samuel has anointed him as the king-to-be: in other words, once he knows that he has been chosen.) Alternatively, it could simply be said that the biblical story, like any myth about the genesis of any people, has to begin somewhere, and with someone: why not with Abraham, in Ur of the Chaldees? Both these arguments are persuasive enough, and they are not incompatible with one another. But they are incompatible with the claims that the Scriptures themselves make on Yahweh's behalf: above all, with the *design* that is insistently imputed to him, from the beginning to the end of the biblical text. He is the active or (if you like) supremely responsible participant in the story of the patriarchs and of the people descended from them; he is the sole and exclusive source of moral order acknowledged in the book. Yet no explanation is given of his most crucial decision; no moral or any other justification is proffered of the most fateful of the choices he makes. At the same time, the book itself makes it clear that to enter into the realm of choices is to enter irrevocably into the realm of morality.

"The Lord sees not as man sees." In some of the biographical narratives, there is a hint that the favored of God might be those who are scorned or overlooked by others. "When the Lord saw that Leah was hated, he opened her womb; but Rachel was barren" (Genesis 29:31). Even David falls into this category; no one thinks to send for him, the youngest son of Jesse, when Samuel comes to the house in search of Saul's successor to the throne. A preference by Yahweh for the downtrodden is more than hinted at in the account of the liberation of the entire people from their bondage in Egypt; while in the codes of law and conduct that are promulgated in Yahweh's name in Exodus, Leviticus, and Deuteronomy, the weakest members of society—the poor, the fatherless, the widow, and the sojourner or stranger—are spoken of with great moral generosity, even with tenderness, as being under his special guardianship. ("Love the sojourner, therefore, for you were sojourners in the land of Egypt." Another form of reciprocity, that must be called.) Eventually, in a development already alluded to in discussing the fall of Jersualem, the prophets who faced the catastrophes of national defeat and exile, and all the hardships of their own calling, were more and more to insist programmatically that God's final election must fall upon the humiliated and the outcast. Yet in developing out of their own tragic situation this systematization or moralization of the way in which Yahweh makes his choices, the prophets, inevitably enough, invoked as precedent his (belated) recollection of his promises to the patriarchs during an earlier period of exile and servitude. And that brings us back, as they intended it to, to the mystery of his initial choice.

It is not surprising that later rabbinical commentators were also to attempt to rationalize the initial choice of Abraham and (some of) his descendants by inventing a series of what might be called justificatory legends about it. It was said, for instance, that Yahweh had offered the yoke of his Law to all the nations of the earth in turn; only Israel had been willing to accept it. It was also said that even as a boy Abraham had distinguished himself by his contempt for idolatry, and by breaking the idols of his father. There is no warrant in the text itself for these stories; in fact, what they betray is a certain unease about there being no warrant for them. . . .

A rather more sophisticated, theological justification for the apparent arbitrariness—or "scandal"—of Yahweh's choice of the people of Israel has been urged with particular insistence by some Christian interpreters: Paul, the ex-Jew, being the very first among them (Romans 9:10–11). As I understand it, the argument goes that if we were to be given a reason for the choice, then the quality of grace it shows would inevitably be diminished or devalued; indeed, to seek for a reason is to attempt to do away with the very notion of God exercising his completely unconstrained will in the matter, which is the only true meaning the word "choice" should have. This is ingenious, and in some ways it actually seems to me closer to what we find in the text than are the rabbinical stories just cited; at least it confronts the fact that we are dealing with an act of unexplained and dangerous favoritism—and one that was at a profound level recognized as such by the biblical writers themselves.

The freedom which Yahweh enjoys is in any case constrained in one most important respect: the one thing he is *not* free to do is to refrain from choosing. At a time when there are only four people on the entire earth—Adam, Eve, and their two sons—he is already engaged in the practice. "And the Lord had regard for Abel and his offering, but for Cain and his offering he had no regard." The consequences of this, supposedly God's very first act of favoritism, are at once shown to be disastrous for both brothers. First it produces envy, then murder, then a man forever on the run. But does Yahweh learn from this experience? Not at all! Once he has begun in this way, he apparently cannot stop. "I will be gracious to whom I will be gracious," he says, with more grimness than grace in Exodus 33:19–20, "and I will show mercy on whom I will show mercy." (The passage is quoted in the Pauline Letter mentioned above.) Everything that follows can be understood as an illustration or elaboration of this ambiguous utterance. Whole peoples are chosen and rejected; the land is chosen and later, in a sense, rejected; so are particular groups and tribes within Israel itself; so are particular places within the land. The record of these events obviously reflects in each case some greater or lesser vicissitude in the history of the nation or in the history of the cult; but it also reveals just how "natural" to the Israelites' conceptions of God was the act of choosing and rejecting, in so many different contexts. This activity is strongly associated, especially in Leviticus, with that ritualistic preoccupation with "holiness" and "separation," with "cleanness" and "uncleanness," in terms of which everything, from the fish in the sea to the days of the calendar, was ultimately to be categorized. That preoccupation, I need hardly add, still looms large in rabbinic Judaism. "I am the Lord your God, who has separated you from the peoples. You shall *therefore* make a distinction between the clean beast and the unclean" (Leviticus 20:24–25).

What makes this God such an inveterate or compulsive chooser? What is it about the act of choosing that reveals his very nature? The answer I am going to suggest shows clearly that in the creation of our fantasies, and hence in the development of our moral lives, "weaknesses" and "strengths" are as inextricably bound up with one another as are "good" impulses and "bad." Yahweh comes into being as a choosing God because, unlike the gods of Egypt or Assyria, say, or even those of Canaan, he is not autochthonous; that is, he is God of a people whose primal historical memory appears to be one of enslavement and homelessness, of searching for a territory, of being without that which all other peoples apparently had. Like the people, he is a wanderer, a God looking for a land—therefore he has to "choose" the land from outside it, just as he had originally to choose or form the people itself.

> For ask now of the days that are past, which were
> before you, since the day that God created man upon
> the earth, and ask from one end of heaven to the other,
> whether such a great thing as this has ever happened
> or was ever heard of. . . . Or has any god ever at-
> tempted to go and take a nation for himself from the
> midst of another nation, by trials, by signs, by wonders,
> and by war, by a mighty hand and an outstretched
> arm, and by great terrors, according to all that the
> Lord your God did for you in Egypt before your eyes?
>
> DEUTERONOMY 4:32, 34

In other words, if it had *not* been said of Yahweh that he had created heaven and earth, if he had not been given "extraterritorial" status from the very outset, he would not have been able to dispose of a land that was not "his," and deal so effectively with the Egyptians, or choose as his own a nation which was still to become a nation.

> Thus you shall say to the house of Jacob, and tell
> the people of Israel: You have seen what I did to the
> Egyptians, and how I bore you on eagles' wings and
> brought you to myself. Now therefore, if you will obey
> my voice and keep my covenant, you shall be my own
> possession among all peoples; for all the earth is mine,
> and you shall be to me a kingdom of priests and a
> holy nation.
>
> EXODUS 19:3–6

And if this was true for the Israelites when they began to keep the record of his deeds, during their time of national independence, it had to be no less true for the prophets when they contemplated the destruction of Jersualem, the burning of his Temple, and the renewed enslavement of his people.

Out of the people's weakness had come his power, including his power to choose; the wider the scope of that power was seen to be, the greater was the glory of those upon whom his choice had fallen—and also the more exposed and vulnerable they felt their position to be. Yahweh had been free to choose Israel, or not, as he wished. Israel, it seemed, had no choice but to be chosen.

CHAPTER FOUR

THE COVENANT

Behold, to the Lord your God belong heaven and the
heaven of heavens, the earth with all that is in it;
yet the Lord set his heart in love upon your fathers
and chose their descendants after them, you above all
peoples, as at this day.

DEUTERONOMY 10:14–15

Imagine writing the history of the people singled out by
that choice and exposed to that love: a history whose purpose is as much to try to secure their future as it is to
record their past. Imagine the sense of awe and responsibility
that must have filled the hearts of those who believed themselves to be directly transcribing the truths revealed to them
by the God of whom they speak: a God of unbridled, unpredictable power, who was the source of all life and death
and was yet capable of feeling love, hatred, anger, jealousy,
and kindness toward his own creations—and acting accord-
ingly. Only if we try to enter wholeheartedly into their
state of mind and the emotional condition that must have
gone with it can we have an inkling of the depths at which
the biblical story took shape, and of the intensities of response that it demanded of its creators.

Perhaps it is the psalmist who most fully opens before
us the possibility of that kind of understanding:

O Lord my God, thou art very great!
Thou art clothed with honor and majesty,
who coverest thyself with light as with a garment,
who hast stretched out the heavens like a tent,
who hast laid the beams of thy chambers on the waters,
who makest the clouds thy chariot,
who ridest on the wings of the wind,
who makest the winds thy messengers, fire and flame
    thy ministers.
Thou didst set the earth on its foundations,
so that it should never be shaken.
Thou didst cover it with the deep as with a garment;
the waters stood above the mountains.
At thy rebuke they fled;
at the sound of thy thunder they took to flight.
The mountains rose, the valleys sank down
to the place which thou didst appoint for them.
Thou didst set a bound which they should not pass,
so that they might not again cover the earth.
. . . .
The trees of the Lord are watered abundantly,
the cedars of Lebanon which he planted.
In them the birds build their nests;
the stork has her home in the fir trees.
The high mountains are for the wild goats;
the rocks are a refuge for the badgers.
Thou hast made the moon to mark the seasons;
the sun knows its time for setting.
Thou makest darkness, and it is night,
when all the beasts of the forest creep forth.
The young lions roar for their prey, seeking their food
    from God.
When the sun rises, they get them away
and lie down in their dens.
Man goes forth to his work and to his labor until the
    evening.

O Lord, how manifold are thy works!
In wisdom hast thou made them all;

the earth is full of thy creatures.
Yonder is the sea, great and wide,
which teems with things innumerable,
living things both small and great.
There go the ships,
and Leviathan which thou didst form to sport in it.

These all look to thee,
to give them their food in due season.
When thou givest to them, they gather it up;
when thou openest thy hand, they are filled with good
    things.
When thou hidest thy face, they are dismayed;
when thou takest away their breath, they die
and return to their dust.
When thou sendest forth thy Spirit, they are created;
and thou renewest the face of the ground.

May the glory of the Lord endure for ever,
may the Lord rejoice in his works,
who looks on the earth and it trembles,
who touches the mountains and they smoke!
PSALM 104:1–9, 16–32

    In this Psalm—a "creation hymn" it has been called by biblical commentators, some of whom believe it to have been adapted from either a Canaanite or an Egyptian original—God's power is described in terms that are on the whole more tender than in many others; but this does nothing to diminish the wonder and reverence which the poem conveys, or the directness with which the poet reveals his unquestioning belief in the full "personhood" of the all-powerful and all-generating deity. Now: imagine that for no reason that has been divulged to you, or that you can divulge to others, your people, and indeed you individually, as a representative of your people, have been chosen by this God to participate in a uniquely close relationship with him;

you have been selected to be the recipient of his particular attention and an exclusive form of his love. You have no choice in the matter: what a diminution of God's power it would be if you did! Surely you would not only exult in the relationship, but would try to protect yourself from some of the possible consequences of being so loved.

Above all, you would want to protect yourself from the prospect of that terrifying love turning away from you— which would mean its turning into a far more terrifying hatred. There is no harmless alternative between love and hatred in such a relationship, no intermediate stage: there never is, with emotions as intense and exclusive as these. All the peoples around you, who have been rejected because you have been chosen, and whom you believe to have suffered because of the favor shown to you, and to be full of hatred and envy as a result, would never permit indifference and anonymity to be your lot, if God's favor should turn from you; it is inconceivable that God himself would permit it, after having so elevated you; you yourself could not tolerate or survive being abandoned by him, once you had known his favor.

How to prevent it? Can it be prevented? How, without declining your chosen status (which in any case you are not free to do), can you try to hold on to what you want from it, and fend off that which you dread?

Considerations as basic as these must be kept in mind if one is to try to understand the overwhelming importance within the Hebrew Scriptures of that for which they have probably been most honored and also most execrated: the presentation of the Law as the direct, unalterable, and all-embracing expression of the will of Yahweh, and the insistence upon a peremptory obedience to it by the people of Israel as the condition for their retaining his love and favor.

That, in essence, is the central clause of the covenant or contract formally entered into between the Israelites and their God, which the Bible tells us was sealed first in the desert under the leadership of Moses, and was renewed thereafter in the flesh of every male child born into the community, as well as in solemn public ceremonies which are reported over and over again in the historical books. At these public ceremonies the original terms of the contract were formally stated again and again. If they, the Israelites, would obey the behests of God, as these are expressed in his commandments and ordinances, then he, the other contracting party, would preserve them in prosperity in the land he had made over to them. If not—well, we have already had more than a glimpse of the alternatives.

Historians of the ancient Near East have shown that the form of the covenant between Yahweh and the people of Israel, as it appears in Exodus, Leviticus, Deuteronomy, and Joshua, follows fairly closely the patterns of treaties concluded in the second and first millennia B.C. between conquering Hittite and Assyrian "great kings" and their vassals; these treaties are in effect acts of submission by the inferior party. One can understand why the bibilical writers should have used such a form in order to express the special relationship they believed they had with their God. What other models were open to them? The fact that Yahweh is not a foreign conqueror but a transcendent and invisible deity; that the treaty imposed by him upon the Israelites governs not only the "foreign policy" of the vassals, which appears to be the case in the parallel, political covenants, but also every detail of the community's life and the cult of the deity himself; that with its accompanying ethical injunctions and elaborate codifications of legal practice this covenant is presented virtually as a constitution for the community which is called into being—such discrepancies between the biblical covenant and those dictated by kings of flesh and blood to their defeated foes must have seemed inconsequential to the Israelites, compared to the appositeness and power of the formal precedents they were drawing upon.*

But there is one feature of the covenant between the Israelites and Yahweh which I would suspect to be quite unlike anything that can be found or even imagined in the comparable international documents; so much so that it seems impossible the Israelites should not have been aware of its significance from a legal or political point of view. What I am referring to is the stress laid upon the *exclusivity* of the covenant between Yahweh and his people. In the political covenants, the subject signatories are of course expressly forbidden from having dealings with other powers, with third parties; but in the nature of the case it is unlikely that the great king himself, the suzerain, the author of the treaty, should tie his own hands in this way. Yet quite apart from the many hundreds of references throughout the Scriptures to the singularity of Yahweh's relationship with Israel, we find specific promises in this regard being given by him in various versions of the covenant itself. "I will take you for my people, and I will be your God" (Exodus 6:7). The mutuality of this aspect of the relationship is hardly less plainly expressed in Leviticus 20:26, in the manner in which a shared "holiness," and hence a shared

---

* The comparison between the biblical covenant and the constitution of a state is one that has often been made. Like a constitution, the covenant is seen as being in itself a kind of legislative act, and also as the source of authority for all the legislation that follows from it. ("I find the Kingdome of God to signifie in most places of Scripture, *a Kingdome properly so named*, constituted by the Votes of the People of Israel in a peculiar manner; wherein they chose God for their King of Covenant made with him, upon God's promising them the possession of the land of Canaan"—Hobbes, *Leviathan*.

"separateness" of deity and people, is spoken of: "You shall be holy to me; for I the Lord am holy, and have separated you from the peoples, that you should be mine." Finally, notice how the "declarations" of the one party to the covenant match formally those of the other, in Deuteronomy 26:17–18: "You have declared this day concerning the Lord that he is your God, and that you will walk in his ways and keep his statutes and his commandments and his ordinances, and will obey his voice; and the Lord has declared this day concerning you that you are a people for his own possession, as he has promised you."

The commandments which God is said to have laid upon the people are gathered together in several different collections in Exodus, Numbers, Deuteronomy, and Leviticus. The most famous compilation of all is of course the Ten Commandments (which are given in two different forms, in Exodus and Deuteronomy—and there is in addition a separate "Ritual Decalogue" elsewhere in Exodus). The other laws and edicts, many of which are believed to be derived ultimately from the Bablyonian Code of Hammurabi, dated about 1730 B.C., cover the widest possible range of topics, and take a variety of forms, from general ethical and moral injunctions to fairly detailed juridical rulings on the ownership of cattle, land, and slaves, as well as questions of divorce, debt, criminal acts, and so forth. There are also scores of successive chapters devoted to cultic matters and the duties of the priesthood. In some cases the distinctions between ethical injunctions, "jurisprudence," and cultic regulations are made fairly clear from their mode of presentation; in others, not at all. (The Ten Commandments, after all, are simultaneously cultic, ethical, and jurisprudential.) The relationship between all the different bodies of law, and the approximate date of each one, have been the subject of much critical and historical labor; so has their relationship to other codes of law within the ancient Near East; so has the elucidation of their "meanings," in terms that range from the anthropological to the allegorical. And it is by extrapolation from these laws that the immensely elaborate corpus of post-biblical, rabbinical law, which produced Orthodox Judaism as it has been known for almost two millennia, claimed to derive its entire authority.

One thing the compilations have in common is that all are said to come directly from Yahweh. Whether the laws are uttered by God to Moses ("And God spoke all these words, saying . . ."), or whether Moses reports God's words to the waiting Israelites ("Now this is the commandments, the statutes, and the ordinances which the Lord your God commanded me to teach to you"), they are all *his*. In this respect no distinction is made between social or economic law on the one hand, and religious law on the other; or between ritual and ethical law. It follows that any transgression of any commandment is nothing less than a rebellion against the express will of God, and is regarded as such within the lawbooks themselves. Provision is made, most notably in Leviticus, for the purging of inadvertent transgressions of the laws governing ritual purity; but apart from certain laws specifically directed toward the priestly class, everything in the lawbooks is presented to the people as a whole. (The Code of Hammurabi, by contrast, is ultimately assigned by the king to the care of a royal successor "who shall be [raised up] in the land"; he is required by Hammurabi to "observe the just words which I have inscribed on my monument.") Furthermore, the Scriptures tell us repeatedly not only that Yahweh's commandments are addressed to the people, but also that they are formally accepted by the people:

> Moses came and told the people all the words of the Lord and all the ordinances; and all the people answered with one voice, and said, 'All the words which the Lord has spoken we will do.'
>
> EXODUS 24:3

> Moses assembled all the congregation of the people of Israel, and said to them, 'These are the things which the Lord has commanded you to do. . . .' Then all the congregation of the people of Israel departed from the presence of Moses. And they came, every one whose heart stirred him, and every one whose spirit moved him, and brought the Lord's offering. . . .
>
> EXODUS 35:1, 20–21

And in return?

> If you walk in my statutes and observe my commandments and do them, then I will give you your rains in their season, and the land shall yield its increase, and the trees of the field shall yield their fruit. And your threshing shall last to the time of vintage, and the vintage shall last to the time for sowing; and you shall eat your bread to the full, and dwell in your land securely. And I will give peace in the land, and you shall lie down, and none shall make you afraid; and I will remove evil beasts from the land, and the sword shall not go through your land. And you shall chase your enemies, and they shall fall before you by the sword. . . . And I will have regard for you and make you fruitful and multiply you, and will confirm my covenant with you. And you shall eat old store long kept, and you shall clear out the old to make way for the new. And I will make my abode among you, and my soul shall not abhor you. And I will walk among you, and will be your God, and you shall be my people. I am the Lord your God, who brought you

forth out of the land of Egypt, that you should not
be their slaves; and I have broken the bars of your
yoke and made you walk erect.

LEVITICUS 26:3–7, 9–13

Now, it may seem (as it did to Hegel, if I have read
Der Geist des Judentums correctly) that so far from Yahweh
having made the Israelites "walk erect," he in fact lifted
the "yoke" of Egyptian slavery from them, and brought
them into the promised land, only in order to impose another yoke on them: that of his unalterable and unquestion-
able will. (It was all that could be done, in Hegel's view,
with a rabble of ex-slaves—and Jews to boot.) The view I
would put forward is, as it were, the very opposite of this.
The centrality given to the covenant Law in the Scriptures
actually represents an attempt by the biblical writers to
put a yoke upon Yahweh. To say that is not merely to
repeat a commonplace in religious-historical writing on the
covenant: namely, that like any other contract it is a two-
way affair, under which God binds himself to the people
as well as the people to God. Nor is it merely to repeat a
little more emphatically the point I made a few pages earlier
about the unprecedented exclusivity of this particular version of a contract between suzerain and vassal. The Sinai
covenant and everything that went with it should be seen
as an all-but-explicit attempt by the biblical writers to pre-
clude the possibility of this inveterate chooser among gods
again exercising his free will, so far as the people of Israel
and "the nations" are concerned. Once was enough. Twice
could only mean disaster. Out of the arbitrariness and in-
scrutableness of the initial choice the biblical writers wanted
to make something predictable and orderly and rational.
Hence in lashing themselves down within the covenant,

and to all its accompanying laws, they hoped to lash down Yahweh too. *Quid pro quo.*

The case parallels in some respects the one presented in the last chapter. There I suggested that because the Israelite traditions were those of weakness and homelessness, they created a God who was powerful enough to "choose" among the nations and the countries of the earth. Having revealed his identity to Moses and the Israelites in the desert, this founder and ruler of the universe, who shows so much partiality among his own creatures, at once enters into a mutually binding arrangement with the people whom he has decided to favor above all others. It cannot be an accident that this arrangement is unmistakably juridical in form; nor can it be accidental that it is made to turn directly upon the acceptance by the people of a whole series of codes of law, for every stipulation of which God himself is supposed to be responsible. At some level the biblical writers knew exactly what they were doing when they made questions of law—law of every kind—so central to the religion of Yahweh. What is more predictable than a contract or a code of law? Laws are codified precisely so that people can know where they stand; they are firm, settled, "objective," public; they are there to be referred to; predictability is of their essence. That is what distinguishes them from the ever-fluctuating whims of rulers—in effect, the only other form of government known to human societies. And could any people have feared this ruler's whim more than the Israelites, who having been its beneficiaries could only be the sufferers should it ever be reversed? Because he had been arbitrary—partial, or unjust, it might be said—in choosing one people above all others, every effort had to be made to ensure that henceforth his rule would be strictly "according to the book."

All this—if I am right—seems to illustrate wonderfully the nature of the dynamic interchange which constantly takes place within us between desire, fantasy, and moral impulse; it is striking evidence of how our loftiest moral impulses can spring from that within ourselves which is most greedily self-preserving—or to put it even more strongly, how those impulses *have* to spring in part from such sources if they are to have any strength at all; if they are to find true nourishment in our innermost natures.

One might think that nothing could be more distant than codes of law, in their public and institutional character, from inward and unconscious acts of "re-insurance" and restitution of the kind I have tried to describe; yet here the relationship appears to be an intimate one. I am not of course saying that any particular ordinance in the various biblical "lawbooks" can be traced back etiologically to considerations of the kind just described. Nor do I need reminding that all societies have to have some more or less elaborate legal system; which means, in turn, that they have to have their own myths describing how their laws came to them. But the tension between the desire to be chosen and the fear of being chosen must help to account for the extraordinary prominence given in the Scriptures both to the Law as the central, nation-building institution and to the idea of it as belonging to Yahweh's domain exclusively.

The same issue can be approached from another angle. Scholars say that a truly original feature of the codes of law in the Scriptures is that, unlike others of that time and place, they are no "respecter of persons." ("You shall not respect persons in judgement"—Deuteronomy 1:17.) Though distinctions are made between freemen and slaves, and between Israelites and strangers, the various codes repeatedly warn judges against the sin of "partiality," and urge them to "hear the great and the small alike." (Again, this can be compared with what is to be found in the Code of Hammurabi, where certain laws apply to "seigniors" and others apply to "commoners," among the people of the land.)

Now, this insistence in the Scriptures upon impartiality in judgment sometimes sits very oddly with the material around it. It certainly does so in the case of the passage from Deuteronomy quoted at the very head of this chapter. There, immediately after declaring in such emphatic terms that he has "set his heart in love" upon the Israelites *above all peoples,*" Yahweh goes on to assert that he himself is *"not partial* and takes no bribes" (10:17). We then have the reference to the fatherless, the widow, and the sojourner or stranger as being under his special care, which has already been alluded to on page 52. In virtually one breath, it seems, he has revealed his favoritism in choosing Israel and set himself up as the very exemplar of impartiality.

How is one to respond to this? One could say simply that the two utterances have little or nothing to do with one another. In the first, speaking of his chosen people, Yahweh appears as the most high God with a mysterious plan for them, to be revealed in the course of their history; in the second he is merely urging upon his people a particular generous example of social law. Alternatively one could say that all that is revealed in the juxtaposition of the two passages is a primitive hypocrisy, ethnocentricity, and absence of logic. My own view is that the relationship between them is more complicated and more interesting than either of these responses suggests. I would argue that they are indeed connected, and indeed contradictory; and that the contradiction is a meaningful one. It is not in spite of his declaration of favoritism toward the Israelites that Yahweh is impelled to insist on impartiality in the treatment of all persons (including strangers) before the law; it is because of it. Having accepted the favor done to them, and meaning to retain it if they possibly can, the Israelites would like everything to be arranged differently—henceforth. Precisely out of their anxiety about God's partiality toward them, and their chosen status, they have proclaimed a principle new to the prevailing notions of justice.

If that is hypocritical—and it is clear why one might think it so—then so are all moral innovations or enlargements of judgment in our own lives and in the history of the race, which are born out of what appear to be wholly self-regarding impulses and anxieties. But if such moral developments are to be really new, where else could they find their origins; and what else could give them nourishment?

Incised in stone ("the tables of testimony"); written in books ("the book of the covenant" or "the book of the law"); placed in or next to the Ark of the Lord (also called "the Ark of the Covenant" or "the Ark of Testimony"); proclaimed aloud in solemn assemblies at seasonal festivals and formally renewed in times of national crisis; growing always in complexity—the Law was eventually to survive the polity it was created to govern and to guide. In a sense it even *became* the polity, after undergoing a process of encyclopedic enlargement, elaboration, and diversification over many hundreds of years. For believing Jews in every part of the world, Talmudic legislation and learning became the means through which they knew themselves to be members of a community with a continuing historic life; even though the community and its life were severed from the land and the cult that had once sustained them.

CHAPTER FIVE

THE REJECTION

The treaty concluded in the seventh century B.C. between the redoubtable Esarhaddon ("king of the world, king of Assyria, son of Sennacherib") and a city ruler by the name of Ramataya included many curses which were suspended on condition of good behavior over the head of Ramataya. Should he go into rebellion, or plot with the king's enemies, or hear disloyal speech and not repeat it, or commit any other such offense, then:

May the great gods of heaven and earth, who inhabit the world, all those that are named in this tablet, strike you down, look with disfavour upon you, curse you angrily with a baleful curse, on earth; may they uproot you from the living, below, may they deprive your spirit of water (libations), may they chase you away from both shade and sunlight so that you cannot take refuge in a hidden corner, may food and drink forsake you, and hunger, want, famine, and pestilence never leave you, may . . . the earth not receive your body for burial, may the bellies of dogs and pigs be your burial place . . . let tar and pitch be your food, donkey urine your drink, naphtha your ointment . . .*

---

* Quoted from *The Ancient Near Eastern Texts Relating to the Old Testament*, edited by James B. Pritchard.

The resemblance between language of this kind and some of what can be found in the covenant passages in Deuteronomy is clear enough. (And it must not be forgotten that the parallel is not merely one of language, but involves also, according to students of such matters, the ordering of the various elements of which the entire covenant is composed: the preamble, the stipulations, the list of witnesses, and so forth.) Deuteronomy 28:20–29, for instance, may in some ways be more eloquent than the passage quoted above, but the burden of its meaning appears to be much the same:

> The Lord will send upon you curses, confusion, and frustration, in all that you undertake to do, until you are destroyed and perish quickly, on account of the evil of your doings, because you have forsaken me. The Lord will make the pestilence cleave to you until he has consumed you off the land which you are entering to take possession of it. The Lord will smite you with consumption, and with fever, inflammation, and fiery heat, and with drought, and with blasting, and with mildew; they shall pursue you until you perish. And the heavens over your head shall be brass, and the earth under you shall be iron. The Lord will make the rain of your land powder and dust; from heaven it shall come down upon you until you are destroyed.
> The Lord will cause you to be defeated before your enemies; you shall go out one way against them, and flee seven ways before them; and you shall be a horror to all the kingdoms of the earth. And your dead body shall be food for all birds of the air, and for the beasts of the earth; and there shall be no one to frighten them away. The Lord will smite you with the boils of Egypt, and with the ulcers and the scurvy and the itch, of which you cannot be healed. The Lord will smite you with madness and blindness and confusion of mind; and you shall grope at noonday, as the blind

grope in darkness, and you shall not prosper in your ways; and you shall be only oppressed and robbed continually, and there shall be no one tohelp you.

However, in the treaty between Esarhaddon and Ramataya, the representative of one state is clearly dictating his terms to the representative of another. Esarhaddon, with the power of his army and empire behind him, is compelling someone who is politically and militarily weaker than himself to accept his will. Hence there is a "real," present, unarguable sanction behind the treaty and the curses it contains: a sanction without which (one might reasonably assume) Ramataya would never have signed it. This is not to say that the curses are therefore devoid of meaning: far from it. Both parties would presumably have been convinced that "the great gods of heaven and earth," of which the treaty speaks, had played their part in elevating Esarhaddon to his position and reducing Ramataya to his; no doubt, also, both of them believed that a degree of magical power, independent of themselves, as it were, resided in the very utterance and inscription of the curses. (Even the tablet on which the treaty was inscribed was evidently regarded as a sacred object: one paragraph warns Ramataya against turning it face downward—"by some trick"—as well as against burning it, drowning it, or burying it in the dust!) But all that said, the terms of the treaty, the very existence of the treaty, *including* the curses, depended wholly upon the arms and the men which the emperor had at his command—and which both he and Ramataya knew he would use if he was provoked to do so.

At his command, it might seem, Yahweh had only the passionate intensity with which the biblical writers projected all their fears, hopes, and bewilderments into him. But the paradoxical result of that very intensity was that he was endowed by them with "real" armies to deploy, too: the armies of the enemies of Israel. Some of the strangest and most powerful passages of writing in the Bible as a whole are those in which the prophets speak, with a mixture of terror and exhilaration, of the nations which God will use to chastise his chosen ones. The more terrifying and implacable they make those nations appear, the greater is the strength they are imputing to Yahweh.

> He will raise a signal for a nation afar off,
> and whistle for it from the ends of the earth;
> and lo, swiftly, speedily it comes!
> None is weary, none stumbles, none slumbers or sleeps,
> not a waistcloth is loose, not a sandal-thong broken;
> their arrows are sharp, all their bows bent,
> their horses' hoofs seem like flint,
> and their wheels like the whirlwind.
> Their roaring is like a lion, like young lions they roar;
> they growl and seize their prey,
> they carry it off, and none can rescue.

Thus Isaiah (5:26–29), speaking in all likelihood of the Assyrians. And Jeremiah, a century and a half later, has somewhat similar things to say about the Babylonians:

> Behold, I am bringing upon you
> a nation from afar, O house of Israel, says the Lord.
> It is an enduring nation,
> it is an ancient nation,
> a nation whose language you do not know,
> nor can you understand what they say.
> Their quiver is like an open tomb,
> they are all mighty men.
>
> 5:15–16

Poetically, psychologically, and (not least) politically, these are remarkable utterances. For Yahweh's sake, the prophets are in effect siding with the enemies of their own people. Some of the conditions and consequences of this will be looked at in the next chapter. However, in order to convey the complexity and the ferocity of the processes involved, I return to the presentation of the covenant in Deuteronomy, and proffer another, much longer passage from that book.

> Because you did not serve the Lord your God with joyfulness and gladness of heart, by reason of the abundance of all things, therefore you shall serve your enemies whom the Lord will send against you, in hunger and thirst, in nakedness, and in want of all things; and he will put a yoke of iron upon your neck, until he has destroyed you. The Lord will bring a nation against you from afar, from the end of the earth, as swift as the eagle flies, a nation whose language you do not understand, a nation of stern countenance, who shall not regard the person of the old or show favour to the young, and shall eat the offspring of your cattle and the fruit of your ground, until you are destroyed; who also shall not leave you grain, wine, or oil, the increase of your cattle or the young of your flock, until they have caused you to perish. They shall besiege you in all your towns, until your high and fortified walls, in which you trusted, come down throughout all your land; and they shall besiege you in all your towns throughout all your land, which the Lord your God has given you. And you shall eat the offspring of your own body, the flesh of your sons and daughters, whom the Lord your God has given you, in the siege and in the distress with which your enemies shall distress you. The man who is the most tender and delicately bred among you will grudge food to his brother, to the wife of his bosom, and to the last of the children who remain to him; so that he will not give to any of them any of the flesh of his children whom he is eating, because he has nothing left him, in the siege and in the distress with which your enemy shall dis-

tress you in all your towns. The most tender and deli-
cately bred woman among you, who would not venture
to set the sole of her foot upon the ground because
she is so delicate and tender, will grudge to the husband
of her bosom, to her son and to her daughter, her
afterbirth that comes out from between her feet and
her children whom she bears, because she will eat them
secretly, for want of all things, in the siege and in
the distress with which your enemy shall distress you
in your towns.

If you are not careful to do all the words of this
law which are written in this book, that you may fear
this glorious and awful name, the Lord your God, then
the Lord will bring on you and your offspring extraordinary afflictions, afflictions severe and lasting, and sick-
nesses grievous and lasting. And he will bring upon
you again all the diseases of Egypt, which you were
afraid of; and they shall cleave to you. Every sickness
also, and every affliction which is not recorded in the
book of this law, the Lord will bring upon you, until
you are destroyed. Whereas you were as the stars of
heaven for multitude, you shall be left few in number:
because you did not obey the voice of the Lord your
God. And as the Lord took delight in doing you good
and multiplying you, so the Lord will take delight in
bringing ruin upon you and destroying you; and you
shall be plucked off the land which you are entering
to take possession of it. And the Lord will scatter you
among all peoples, from one end of the earth to the
other; and there you shall serve other gods, of wood
and stone, which neither you nor your fathers have
known. And among these nations you shall find no
ease, and there shall be no rest for the sole of your
foot; but the Lord will give you there a trembling heart,
and failing eyes, and a languishing soul; your life shall
hang in doubt before you; night and day you shall
be in dread, and have no assurance of your life. In
the morning you shall say, 'Would it were evening!'

and at evening you shall say, 'Would it were morning!'
because of the dread which your heart shall fear, and
the sights which your eyes shall see.

28:47–67

Many readers will perhaps respond to this with a degree
of distaste, or even of shock, or possibly of defensive amuse-
ment—all of which might be a kind of backhanded tribute
to the imaginative vividness of the writing. If one looks
closely at the whole passage, however, one sees that its
vividness is not just a matter of so many sharply visualized
details. Overall the passage is in fact thematic to a quite
extraordinary degree, however much in it may have been
borrowed from other sources; and its images are organically
related to the overmastering preoccupations or obsessions
of the writers: to the entire "plot," indeed, of which I have
been speaking. Utterly different though it is in style and
intention, the passage illustrates and helps to justify some
of the critical terms used in analyzing the account of the
fall of Jerusalem in Chapter One of this book; it also illumi-
nates the discussion of some of the topics raised there and
in other chapters.

For example, I referred in the first chapter to the almost
punning, to-and-fro movement of vision and expression
characteristic of the biblical writers; this was associated with
the notion of a merciless, endless reciprocity which seemed
to lie at the heart of their view of the divinity and his
dealings with the world. That ironic view of the dynamics
of history, with its eager yet terrified expectation that all
men will in time know the exact reversal or inversion of
whatever conditions they have previously suffered or enjoyed, can be seen at its starkest in the figure with which
the passage opens. Like all instances of "poetic justice," it
reads like an unspeakably bitter joke: *"Because you did*

not serve the Lord your God with joyfulness and gladness of heart, by reason of the abundance of all things, *therefore you shall serve your enemies whom the Lord will send against you,* in hunger and thirst, in nakedness, and in want . . ."

Tit for tat. There is a repetition of this effect later: "And *as* the Lord took delight in doing you good . . . *so* the Lord will take delight in bringing ruin upon you . . ." But we can see a more savage and elaborate development of these ideas in the references to the different crops which are mentioned in the passage: grain, wine, oil, cattle, fruit . . . and one crop of quite another kind. The issue at stake here is that of the "inheritance" by a conquering people of the goods and labors of others; something which was discussed in Chapter Two. In this case it is "the nation of stern countenance" who will be the lucky inheritors of the land, as the Israelites once were, and who "shall eat the offspring of your cattle and the fruit of your ground." But we do not realize the full, hideous import of all this, or even of the word "offspring," until we come to the description of the cannibalism of the starving Israelite men and women whose crops have been taken away from them. What are they eating? Or rather: whom are they eating? The answer is: the very "crops" for whose benefit they had raised all their other crops—the children who they had assumed would in the ordinary course of things inherit their labors.

Another familiar theme which recurs here, obviously and inevitably, is the idea of the people being "plucked off" the land as the Canaanites were, and being driven into exile. (The Israelites were supposed to be entering the land at the time these warnings were ostensibly written: the Book of Deuteronomy purports to contain the last directions given by Moses to the Children of Israel, just before their entry into the promised land and his death outside it.) One should also note the recurrence of the threat to visit on the Israelites "the diseases of Egypt." Like all other favors done for the Israelites by God, which thereafter hung over them like a threat, the plagues of Egypt were much in the minds of the biblical writers, not only as a condign punishment for their Egyptian slavemasters, but also as a possibility to which they were forever exposed. The plagues are mentioned several times in Deuteronomy; in Exodus 15:26, God promises that if the people keep his commandments he "will put none of the diseases upon [them] which I put upon the Egyptians; for I the Lord am your *healer.*" And in Leviticus 26:21, we find, soon after a reference to the deliverance from Egypt: "Then if you walk contrary to me, and will not hearken to me, I will bring more plagues upon you, sevenfold as many as your sins."

All these threats or curses, it is true, are presented as if they are conditional in nature; they are like the sanctions invoked by Esarhaddon against Ramataya should he break the terms of the covenant into which he has entered. Moreover, a series of blessings is offered to the people by way of securing a balance of forces in the text. If they obey God's laws, it is said over and over again, they will be preserved and upheld. "All the peoples of the earth," they are told in the selfsame chapter of Deuteronomy, "shall see that you are called by the name of the Lord; and they shall be afraid of you. And the Lord will make you abound in prosperity, in the fruit of your body, and in the fruit of your cattle, and in the fruit of your ground, within the land which the Lord swore to your fathers to give you" (28:10–11). It is up to the people, the text would have us believe, to choose. Having chosen them over their heads,

God now gives them a choice of their own: literally a choice between life and death. "I have set before you life and death, blessing and curse; therefore choose life, that you and your descendants may live" (30:19).

The trouble is that by the time this choice was offered to the people, one must assume it had already been effectively foreclosed. Indeed, one must go further: that was *why* it was ostensibly offered to them. In other words—the observation is a commonplace—what is presented as a "choice" can more plausibly be thought of as an explanation of an event which either has already taken place or is about to take place. It is *post facto;* or to use another and more expressive Latin phrase which scholars apply to writing of this kind, it is *vaticinium ex eventu:* prophecy from, or out of, the event. Certainly, some of the materials in the extract from Deuteronomy are older than others; but if we read it as a whole, and within the context of all that is around it, and if we pay close attention to the words used in it, we are entitled to draw conclusions about the kind of invasion envisaged by the writers: above all, in their striking references to a nation *"from afar . . .* a nation of stern countenance."* Like Jeremiah, who uses some of the same words, Deuteronomy is speaking explicitly here of the army of a great empire; not of the threats posed by the neighbors of the Israelites in or around Canaan itself. Hence the reference to the distance from which this nation comes. Anyone who has studied Assyrian and Babylonian reliefs which depict the armies of these empires engaged in sieges, battles, and the sack of conquered cities will recognize the "stern countenances" of which the Deuteronomist speaks.

No wonder that whereas the summary of blessings in the climactic chapter of the book runs from verses 1 to 15, the curses run from verses 16 to 68; the curses thus take up about four times as much space as the blessings. In this respect Yahweh reveals himself to be hardly any more generous as a potential dispenser of favors than all those kings in the vassal treaties mentioned above, who are also, inevitably, much freer with their threats and curses than they are with their promises. No wonder, too, that there is nothing random or gratuitous about the particular nightmares invoked in the Deuteronomic curses; their thematic cohesiveness is precisely their point.*

The fact is that while the nature of the threats from Yahweh change according to the circumstances in which the people of Israel find themselves at different periods, he has always been perceived as a source of danger to them. Before they ever arrived in Canaan, when they were still wandering in the desert, he could simply threaten, as he does in various places in Exodus, to "consume" them; to "strike them with pestilence"; to "blot out their name from under heaven"; to "disinherit" them and start all over again with a more docile people. After they had come into possession of the land, other measures were open to him. We have just seen what some of these were imagined to be. All were conceived of as the ultimate sanctions which this suzerain could devise against the stubbornly disobedient and faithless vassals to whom he had once shown such

---

* Most scholars assume that the central core of Deuteronomy is the "lost" law book, whose discovery is recorded in the reign of King Josiah; a discovery which was used by the king and his high priest as the occasion for the solemn, public renewal of the covenant with Yahweh. The date 622 B.C. is usually given for this event: i.e., a hundred years *after* the complete destruction by the Assyrians of the northern kingdom of Israel, and fifty years before the fall of Jerusalem to the Neo-Babylonians. The king and his priests may indeed have hoped that the ceremony of renewal—together with the centralization of the worship of Yahweh in Jerusalem, which the book proposes—would appease God, turn away potential invaders, and avert from themselves the fate that had fallen upon the sister kingdom of the north. We know that these measures did not succeed. So did the people who compiled the final version of Deuteronomy.

favor. They were to blame. They had let him down. They had broken the terms of the covenant. They deserved what they were getting.

The very act of telling the story committed the biblical writers to this view of events; it was the only possible view for those who believed the history of God's relations with his people to be worth transcribing. Who, after all, would want to tell or preserve the story of a god who betrayed his people (Moses had warned Yahweh that he would be accused of betraying the Israelites if he "consumed" them in the desert*); or of a god who misled them; or of a god who proved, when the showdown came, weaker than other gods?

The result is a highly unusual form of "narrative compulsion." The events that were threatening to destroy the Israelite kingdoms had to be interpreted in terms of the myth. But the interpretation which the prophets and historians agreed upon—the accusation of dire sinfulness against the Israelites—alone made the record of the events worth keeping. Without it no one would have bothered. In the historical books Yahweh is said to punish his people by means of the invading strangers chiefly because of their habit of going after strange gods; in the prophetic books he is provoked not only by that sin but also by a host of other

---

* And the Lord said to Moses, 'I have seen this people, and behold, it is a stiff-necked people; now therefore let me alone, that my wrath may burn hot against them and I may consume them; but of you I will make a great nation.'

But Moses besought the Lord his God, and said, 'O Lord, why does thy wrath burn hot against thy people, whom thou hast brought forth out of the land of Egypt with great power and with a mighty hand? Why should the Egyptians say, "With evil intent did he bring them forth, to slay them in the mountains, and to consume them from the face of the earth"? Turn from thy fierce wrath, and repent of this evil against thy people. . . .' And the Lord repented of the evil which he thought to do to his people.

EXODUS 32:9–12, 14

moral failings—pride, greed, cruelty, and so forth. As far as the writers are concerned, these private transactions between the people and their God *become* the "events" that really matter; the rest, all that we might think of as the true subject of any historical record, the marching armies and burning cities, are mere reflex. Or "superstructure."

The familiarity of the result should not blind us to its singularity. The dramatic and psychological consequences of making the people responsible for the downfall of Israel and Judah were of a far-reaching kind. But before going on to consider them in more detail, we must be careful not to take for granted another familiar element in the drama: that of Yahweh's jealousy, his utter intolerance of any tendency on the part of his people to worship other gods. In the context of a drama of choice and rejection, what does this characteristic mean? It means that Yahweh is assumed to know *from within*, like his people, what it is like to suffer the fear of being passed over. He knows the privileges and the agonies of his own solitude, of the "separation" he has imposed on himself, as well as on his people. He experiences all the dread of a lover who can never be certain that his love is wholly and exclusively reciprocated, and that whatever he gets from her will be all that she has to give.

No wonder that one of the favorite figures used by the prophets to describe God's relations with Israel is that of a faithful lover to a harlot-like spouse. The metaphor derives a special effectiveness from the fact that sacred prostitution was institutionalized in many of the rival cults to that of Yahweh. It also provides an example of the way in which a conviction that one is acting or speaking on the side of virtue can license an indulgence in fantasies that virtue itself would ordinarily compel one to forswear. (Other examples of this will be coming up shortly.) There is nothing in the Scriptures that more closely resembles pornography— certainly not the erotic poems of the Song of Songs—than the ravings of Jeremiah and Ezekiel on the subject, with their talk of lewd harlotries and lusty stallions and skirts lifted over faces; of "members like those of asses," and "issue like those of horses," and the pressing of "young breasts."

All this may seem a laborious, if rather picturesque, confirmation of the obvious truth that a single God could tolerate no rivals. But for most of the writers, most of the time, Yahweh's jealous, husbandly qualities stood out all the more sharply because he was often presented as being rather tolerant, in a contemptuous fashion, of other gods for other peoples. *Autres pays, autres dieux* seems to be his attitude, as far as they were concerned. But Israel was different. She was the solitary possession of this solitary God. On her he had to take a boundless revenge for any infidelity or wrongdoing. What was she without him? And he without her?

CHAPTER SIX

THE REJECTION (Continued)

The story told is thus quite clear. The people anger Yahweh by following other gods and (at least as far as the prophets' view of events is concerned) by committing a host of other moral sins. Thereupon Yahweh rejects them. Again and again in the prophetic books and the Psalms one finds words variously translated as "reject," "abandon," "give up," "cast off," and so forth used to describe and to explain Yahweh's treatment of the people during their time of adversity. "Hast thou utterly forsaken us?" asks the poet of Lamentations (5:22), and a number of voices reply more or less as Jeremiah does: "The Lord has forsaken them" (6:30) "Who," the Second Isaiah asks in a rather more elaborate fashion, "gave up Jacob to the spoiler and Israel to the robbers?" and promptly answers that question with yet another: "Was it not the Lord against whom we have sinned?" (42:24). The horrendous punishments of conquest and exile are implicit in the initial act of rejection; they are seen as its working through into the realm of human deed, of historical fact.

What this amounts to is an internalization of the disastrous processes of the history the writers had to confront. Instead of looking on the Aramaeans or Assyrians or Babylonians as independently motivated peoples with their own national or imperial ends to pursue, they transformed them into the involuntary participants in a drama of which they knew nothing. Though all these enemies of Israel may have imagined they had their own reasons for their actions, in fact—that is, in terms of the biblical writers' sense of fact— they were merely acting out roles allotted to them by a deity of whose existence they were unaware, and over whose decisions they had no control whatever. Outwardly the Israelites may have appeared to be a defeated people, a people for whom everything seemed lost. Yet their actions, and their actions alone, were all that mattered, ultimately. They were subject to Yahweh, of course; but there is a not so hidden sense in which he was subject to them. It was the manner in which they comported themselves that determined the nature of his response to them, and to all the other nations he had at his command.

If it was a consolation to the biblical writers to believe the people of Israel possessed such power, no doubt they also found consolation in the belief that they had at their disposal an understanding of events that went far beyond that of their opponents. Moreover, they were in a position to expect that if the people purged its guilt in the eyes of Yahweh, then a revolutionary change in their circumstances would miraculously take place. The mighty enemies of Israel would be able to prevent such a change as little as they had in truth been able to claim credit for their victories.

A few pages previously, I said that some of the strangest writing in the Scriptures is that in which the prophets describe to their own people, with a kind of holy, retributive glee, the armed power of Israel's enemies. No less strange are the closely related passages in which the writers "take over" on Yahweh's behalf the armies which were invading their country, and besieging their cities, and destroying or enslaving their countrymen, and present them as nothing more than unwitting, helpless instruments in his hands. Again, just two examples will have to serve for a great many others. The first is from Isaiah, the second from Jeremiah.

> Ah, Assyria, the rod of my anger, the staff of my fury!
> Against a godless nation I send him,
> and against the people of my wrath I command him,
> to take spoil and seize plunder,
> and to tread them down like the mire of the streets.
> . . . .
> Shall the axe vaunt itself over him who hews with
>   it,
> or the saw magnify itself against him who wields it?
> As if a rod should wield him who lifts it,
> or as if a staff should lift him who is not wood!
>
>   10:5–6, 15

> 'Therefore thus says the Lord of hosts: Because you have not obeyed my words, behold, I will send for all the tribes of the north, says the Lord, and for Nebuchadrezzar the king of Babylon, my servant, and I will bring them against this land and its inhabitants, and against all these nations round about; I will utterly destroy them, and make them a horror, a hissing, and an everlasting reproach.'
>
>   25:8–9

In the lines following immediately upon this passage from Jeremiah, these same Babylonians, who are described here as nothing more than the instruments or servants of Yahweh, are then singled out for special and terrible punishment for having acted as they did. As with innumerable other passages in the same strain, the fact that their crimes against Yahweh's people were committed at Yahweh's direct behest appears to be promptly forgotten:

> Then after seventy years are completed, I will punish
> the king of Babylon and that nation, the land of the
> Chaldeans, for their iniquity, says the Lord, making
> the land an everlasting waste. I will bring upon that
> land all the words which I have uttered against it,
> everything written in this book, which Jeremiah proph-
> esied against all the nations. For many nations and
> great kings shall make slaves even of them; and I will
> recompense them according to their deeds and the
> work of their hands.
>
> 25:12–14

The prophecy here about the punishment of Babylon may
have been written in after the triumph of the Persian emperor Cyrus over the Babylonians: the reference to the
"book," or "scroll," of Jeremiah, as to a completed work,
is a suggestive one; and the error in chronology (the Babylonians in fact enjoyed their triumph over the Israelites for
about fifty years, not seventy) does not seem to me of much
consequence. On the other hand, the verses may represent
an inspired, hopeful guess made before the event. However
that may be, the most striking thing about the passage in
this context is its reference to God's recompensing the Babylonians for "their deeds and the work of their hands." *Their*
deeds, did you say? The work of *their* hands?

Questions like these may rise to the lips of the modern
reader; the ancient writers apparently felt neither the need
nor the temptation to ask them. Note also the application
to the Babylonians here of the law of historical reciprocity
or reversibility—which clearly does not apply only to the
fortunes of the Israelites. How could it? If one side goes
up, the other must come down.

Given the helplessness of the historians and prophets
of Israel in the face of enemies so much more powerful

than themselves, one can see just how comforting the myth of Yahweh's anger must have been. The gains, psychologically speaking, in telling the history of the people in these terms are evident. However, the price exacted, psychologically speaking once again, is also a high one. I am not thinking here merely of the fact that anyone who does not share the writers' beliefs must see this version of events as a retreat from reality, a substitute for reality, a self-blinding by its authors to what is actually happening to them. That is all true enough; but it is not a truth that takes one very far. All stories are made up in order to provide us with a retreat from reality; yet paradoxically, it would be impossible for us to confront reality if we did not habitually make such retreats from it. No, in speaking of the price exacted by this particular story, I want to say something quite specific about the quality of the ideas and emotions engaged by it.

The first point to notice is that if the story of the rejection by Yahweh of his people is indeed an internalization by the biblical writers of certain ineluctable historical facts, it is as well an act of self-rejection on their part. At any rate, in telling the story in these terms they committed themselves to blaming and to fiercely rejecting those people, their fellow Israelites, their own kinsmen, whom they felt to be responsible for the disasters that had come upon the nation as a whole. Now, a misfortune which is regarded simply as a misfortune is quite a different thing from one which we consider to have arisen through a fault of our own, or a fault of those who are closest to us. The misfortunes for which we or they are responsible are much harder to bear than the other kind, as each of us no doubt has reason painfully to know; they can and usually do lead to a hysteria of recrimination against those within the family whom we believe to have been chiefly at fault—as the members of our families also have reason painfully to know.

There is a great deal of this understandable but unpleasant emotion in the prophetic books. What could be expected of Aramaeans and Assyrians and suchlike peoples, other than that they should be the enemies of Israel? But that the most dangerous enemies of Israel should be within Israel; that their misdeeds should involve all Israelites in a common ruin with them; and that the disasters they have brought about should be the result of a deliberate perversity and viciousness of temperament on their part—all this is unendurable. Especially *when you told them so* and they would not listen.

> For twenty-three years, from the thirteenth year of Josiah the son of Amon, king of Judah, to this day, the word of the Lord has come to me, and I have spoken persistently to you, but you have not listened. You have neither listened nor inclined your ears to hear, although the Lord persistently sent to you all his servants the prophets, saying, 'Turn now, every one of you, from his evil way and wrong doings.'
>
> JEREMIAH 25:3–5

Do not such people deserve everything they are going to get? Are you not entitled to imagine in the greatest possible detail the punishments that are quite properly coming their way? Is not the pain you feel in picturing these punishments a warrant for the pleasure you take in them—and vice versa?

It is impossible to assess how much guilt the scriptural interpretation of the history of Israel produced in its original audiences; or how much guilt it has helped to foster among Jews and others since. (Obviously it is relevant here that both Judaism and Christianity are religions in which ideas of guilt and atonement, of a very different kind in each case, play a prominent part.) What is not so difficult to judge is the degree to which certain vindictive and aggressive impulses within the writers were intensified by the fact that they had made their own people wholly responsible for the defeats suffered by Israel. The prophetic writers indulged freely in fantasies of the terrible comeuppance the external enemies of Israel were one day going to receive; much impotent aggression and hatred were vented in that way. But fulminations against the people of Israel provided the authors with a more immediate and more plausible substitute for the endlessly deferred revenge they looked forward to against other nations. (Not that the prophets are all alike in the way they write of these matters; I am speaking here of an overall impression rather than of one or another particular case.) Everything they said about Israel was justified by the manifestly unhappy plight of the people, and by the threats hanging over its future. Whatever might still be in store for the enemies of Israel, at least this much of the prophets' warnings could not be gainsaid. The position of the people was quite as desperate as they declared it to be.

> Therefore, as the tongue of fire devours the stubble,
> and as dry grass sinks down in the flame,
> so their root will be as rottenness,
> and their blossom go up like dust;
> for they have rejected the law of the Lord of hosts,
> and have despised the word of the Holy One of Israel.
> Therefore the anger of the Lord was kindled against
> his people,
> and he stretched out his hand against them and smote
> them,
> and the mountains quaked;
> and their corpses were as refuse in the midst of the
> streets.

For all this his anger is not turned away
and his hand is stretched out still.

ISAIAH 5:24-25

Often, in fact, the prophets appear quite directly to be giving aid and comfort to the enemy rather than to their own kin; to be lending their support to the conquering armies of the greatest imperial powers of the day rather than to their beleaguered victims. I am not overlooking the messages of consolation which the prophets also offered to their people; nor denying that in some of the books, especially those of Jeremiah and the First Isaiah, one can discern the lines of serious political arguments between opposing factions in the palace as how best to respond to the threats which the Judean kingdom had to face at different times. Nor, finally, am I simply accusing the prophets, or some of them, of spreading "alarm and despondency" at times of acute crisis: something which was a crime, it is worth remembering, even in a country with so strongly libertarian a tradition as Great Britain, during the last World War.

The problem goes deeper than all this. Because of their conviction that *only* the wrongdoings of the people of Israel could have brought their misfortunes upon them, the prophets in effect had no choice but to "back" the stronger side in the international embroilments in which the Israelite monarchies were involved. That is both the consequence and the precondition of their insistence that the armies attacking Israel were the executioners of the wrath of Yahweh. Commentators have often referred to the "theological pragmatism" of the Hebrew Scriptures—by which they mean the belief that God rewarded with worldly success those who followed his precepts, and punished those who did not, and that one could easily establish to which category any ruler or group belonged by seeing whether it prospered or failed in its endeavours. It has been less often remarked that this kind of pragmatism could lead to the adoption of the attitude that whoever was victorious or politically supreme at any moment owed his position to the will of Yahweh, and that it was therefore idle or presumptuous to oppose him.

Everyone tells us that the Israelite prophets are to be revered for their stubborn refusal to acknowledge any authority other than that of their God, and hence for their readiness to undergo any sufferings for the sake of the witness they bore. We know also that they attacked the rich and powerful among their own people: those who (in the words of Amos) dwelt in "houses of ivory" and "turned away the needy at the gate." How then can they be accused of an excessive subservience to worldly power? The paradox can be resolved in this way: the one thing the prophets were never subdued or impressed by was *Israelite* power. The political power of the Assyrians or Babylonians was quite another matter in their eyes. It was so imposing, it was so catastrophic in its effects, it could be dealt with only by temporarily assimilating or absorbing it into the power of Yahweh. Once that had been accomplished, it became possible for the prophets to look forward to Yahweh's eventual separation of himself from the doings of these empires, and his rejection and destruction of them. The prophets could also claim that until this came to pass, God's favored ones could be recognized by the chastisements he visited upon them. And if that appeared to be an inversion of the natural order of things—well, one inversion would be bound to lead to another, ultimately.

In more than one context we have seen selfish or aggressive instincts transformed into institutionalized moral precepts and attitudes of an altruistic or a generous kind. Some of the Deuteronomic and prophetic writings present a rather similar process taking place in reverse. The instinct to blame and the impulse to punish are licensed by the conviction of the writers that they are speaking on behalf of God and in the name of his justice, and by the knowledge that they are addressing their own kinsfolk, whose ultimate welfare it is self-evident (to them) they have at heart. This development should be no more surprising to us than its "benign" counterpart.

I would go further still. Just as the writers' accusatory and punitive emotions toward their own people provided them with an outlet for their helpless rage against the foreign conquerors, so it seems to me likely that these emotions were also an outlet for displaced resentment against a God whose power and righteousness they were desperately anxious to assert. All those cries and pleas to him, all those expressions of subservience to him, all those exhortations to the people to worship him as he demanded they should, so that he might relent, and bring the torments of conquest, despoliation, and exile to an end—it is indeed difficult to imagine them being uttered cost-free, so to speak; without some diversion of unadmitted anger and resentment from him toward a softer, more available, less dangerous target.

However, one does find a few places, a very few places, in which there is an outright declaration of innocence by the writers on behalf of their people, and hence an explicit or implicit suggestion that God is acting neither justly nor according to his word. As in the following Psalm:

> Thou has made us like sheep for slaughter,
> and hast scattered us among the nations.
> Thou hast sold thy people for a trifle,
> demanding no high price for them.

Thou hast made us the taunt of our neighbors,
the derision and scorn of those about us

. . . .

All this has come upon us,
though we have not forgotten thee,
or been false to thy covenant.
Our heart has not turned back,
nor have our steps departed from thy way,
that thou shouldst have broken us in the place of jack-
    als,
and covered us with deep darkness.

44:11–13, 17–19

Admittedly, this Psalm is regarded by many scholars as a late one: they believe it was composed during the persecutions of the Jews by the Seleucid Greeks who ruled Palestine during the fourth and third centuries B.C. If this is true, it may help to explain the candor with which the poet expresses his sentiments, for at that time pious Jews were being persecuted precisely because they clung so tenaciously to the precepts of their faith. But one can recognize something resembling the sentiments of that Psalm in passages of even so heartbrokenly submissive a work as the Book of Lamentations, to which a much earlier date is usually given.

The Lord has become like an enemy,
he has destroyed Israel;
he has destroyed all its palaces,
laid in ruins its strongholds;
and he has multiplied in the daughter of Judah
mourning and lamentation.

. . . .

The Lord determined to lay in ruins
the wall of the daughter of Zion;
he marked it off by the line;
he restrained not his hand from destroying;

he caused rampart and wall to lament,
they languish together.
Her gates have sunk into the ground;
he has ruined and broken her bars;
her king and princes are among the nations;
the law is no more,
and her prophets obtain
no vision from the Lord.

                                        2:5, 8–9

The Book of Lamentations was to occupy a place in the interpretation of the "Old" Testament as a foreshadowing in every particular, and on a variety of levels, of the story of Jesus. For a number of obvious reasons, all hints in the Hebrew Scriptures at the possibility of an undeserved or guiltless suffering, either on a national scale or among individuals, became of great importance in the development of the Christian Bible. I do not want to preempt the discussion of this subject in later chapters; for the moment I will simply cite two famous instances, from Psalms 22 and 69, which were used to great effect by the Gospel writers in their accounts of the crucifixion of Jesus. ("My God, my God, why has thou forsaken me? . . . A company of evildoers encircle me; they have pierced my hands and feet— I can count all my bones—they stare and gloat over me; they divide my garment among them, and for my raiment they cast lots"—Psalm 22:1, 16–18. "I looked for pity, but there was none; and for comforters, but I found none. They gave me poison for food, and for my thirst they gave me vinegar to drink"—Psalm 69:20–21.) For many centuries "matching" passages like these were regarded as irrefutable proof that the Christian revelation was indeed a miraculous, foreordained fulfillment of the promises in the Hebrew Scriptures. When the authorities in various countries during the Middle Ages staged public debates between Christian theologians and unwilling Jewish rabbis conscripted to speak on behalf of their coreligionists, passages like these were used by the Christians as their trump card.

From the Christian point of view, an even more important text of this kind is the famous and mysterious Chapter 53 of Isaiah, in which a wholly innocent figure, "despised and rejected by men, a man of sorrows, and acquainted with grief," is said to bear "the sins of many and [make] intercession for the transgressors." More books, perhaps, have been written about this than about any other single chapter in the Hebrew Scriptures. Christians have traditionally seen it, together with the related group of "Suffering Servant" poems, as one of the most compelling prophecies of the life and death of Jesus, and of the salvation that was to come through him; Jews have regarded the figure as an embodiment of the tribulations borne by the people of Israel as a whole. (A more sophisticated notion of prophecy, incidentally, has seen Jesus as knowingly and willingly taking upon himself the role of the Suffering Servant, once he had determined to go up to Jerusalem.) The insistence in Chapter 53 not only on the entire guiltlessness of this figure but also on his capacity to make *others* "whole" through the chastisements he endures is without parallel in the Hebrew Scriptures, so far as I know; the insistence on his eventual triumph is not. "He shall prolong his days; the will of the Lord shall prosper in his hand; he shall see the fruit of the travail of his soul and be satisfied" (10–11).

CHAPTER SEVEN

RENEWAL

After rejection—renewal and restoration. In terms of the story the development was not merely logical or desirable; it was absolutely indispensable. For what would be the point—it has to be asked again, though in a different context from last time—of *telling* the story if it was simply to end with God's rejection of his guilty people, and with their being "vomited out" forever from the land he had given them? To whom, in that case, would the story be addressed? Only the enemies of Israel would then have been able to read it; and they would have derived from it not religious and moral instruction, but pleasure merely. They would have seen it as a tale about a people who were so rebellious, so ungrateful, so immoral, and (incidentally) so stupid, that even their own God was in the end forced to turn away from them, after having incited others to enslave them and pillage their country, on his behalf.

But there again—in saying that I have touched on what is most ironic about the fate of the Hebrew Scriptures over the succeeding millennia. They did indeed become the property of the enemies of Israel. Because of the "Christianization" of the promises to the Israelites which appear in the Scriptures, it *did* come about that the Bible was believed to reveal about the people of Israel no more and no less than I have just said. In the Christian version of the tale, it is true, the final abandonment of the Israelites by God took place only after he had carried out his promise to send them a redeemer, against whose very person they then proceeded to commit an intolerable provocation. The ultimate instruments of God's wrath in this version of the story were the Romans, who destroyed Jerusalem and the rebuilt Temple with a thoroughness which outdid even that of their Babylonian predecessors.

However, there is a further irony to note here. This Christian fulfillment or denouement of the biblical story was itself dependent upon the ideas of a national renewal and restoration which we are about to look at now. They provided not only a context for the narratives of the torment and eventual triumph of Jesus, but also a direct model for them. While all the curses of the prophets against Israel for its obstinacy and blindness were applied by Christian interpreters to the actual, living people, everything that had been said sympathetically about their misfortunes was understood to have been said allegorically or prophetically about Jesus; the same was true of the promises of a messianic redeemer; the same was true, again, of every description of the glorious reversion to come.

The relationship between the promise of renewal and the very existence of the scriptural story is in fact another example of what I earlier called "narrative compulsion." If the writers and their editors had not believed that God would renew his promise to the defeated and demoralized people of Israel, restore the covenant he had made with them, and lead them back to their land, they would not have carried out their respective tasks. Quite simply, there would have been no tasks for them to carry out. The story is intended to help "bring about" certain events; in consequence it is *itself* brought about.

However, there is one important distinction to be made between those features of the story which have already been discussed and the theme of renewal to be dealt with in this chapter and the next. Until now I have been writing about a record which was chiefly concerned with presenting and explaining events that were believed by the writers to be in the past. (This applies as much to the appearance of God before Moses, say, as to the conquest of the land of Canaan.) Now I am about to write of their record of events which they knew had not yet happened—a record which they compiled, indeed, in order to make them happen. In other words, the passionately imaginative constructions still to be discussed have something of a thaumaturgic rather than an explanatory function. Some of the differences between these two kinds of writing will become clear in what follows.

The prophecies in question are mostly those produced before the Babylonian exile. (An exception are Chapters 40–66 of Isaiah, about half of which are believed to have been written about 540 B.C., when the Persian emperor Cyrus permitted the return to Jerusalem of a group of the exiles; and the other half later still.) This means that I am chiefly interested in classical, this-worldly prophecy, and not in the apocalyptic, other-worldly visions of which there are a few examples in the Hebrew Scriptures—in Daniel, for example—and many more in the Apocrypha and elsewhere. Those belong to a later period in the history of the land and the people.* The distinction between proph-

---

* Among the characteristic features of a full-blown apocalypse are visions of a final judgment, and of cosmic warfare between the forces of good and evil;

ecy and apocalypse is indispensable; yet it should be remembered that there are "borderline" writings in almost every prophetic book. In any case, if one has read literally certain metaphors which appear in the prophecies, and if one has read metaphorically certain literal statements in them—as the writing often seems to invite one to do—how can one then securely distinguish between this world and another, wholly remade version of it, which has yet to be unveiled? It is important to remember, too, that both prophecy and apocalypse emerge from conditions which the writers find intolerable and which they dream of seeing convulsively reversed.

What does such a reversal involve? Inevitably, somewhat different things for different writers, depending on their individual temperaments and on the particular historical conjunctures out of which they write. But there are certain expectations which appear in one form or another in almost

---

allegorical beasts and figures set against fantastic landscapes and heavenscapes; numerological clues to the date and order of the events described, which are connected in riddling fashion to actual historical personages and occurrences— all of this amounting to an ultimate, not to say orgasmic, settling of accounts for everyone and with everyone. Apocalypse has often been described as the "child" of classical or historical prophecy—and so it is: the bastard child, the child of woe and of hope grown sick, and of dreams of revenge become so frantic the earthly Jerusalem and circumjacent lands could no longer provide a stage big enough for their enactment. Classical prophecy was itself born largely as a response or resistance to defeat and despair; in the apocalyptic writings Yahweh's great scheme of redemption for Israel became cosmically enlarged, and was inextricably mixed up with elements of which the prophecies are almost entirely innocent: astrology, angelogy, demonology, doctrines of the afterlife and of a last judgment of souls.

In the view of most scholars, mainstream Judaism was to turn its back decisively on writing of this kind after the failure of the last Jewish revolt against Rome in A.D. 135. (The rebels, like their equally ill-fated predecessors of seventy years before, were believed to have been misled by their reading in an apocalyptic spirit what they imagined to be certain portents favorable to their cause.) The success of Christianity, which was in its early stages a truly apocalyptic religion, also did much to make the rabbis suspicious of the genre. However, it is true that some apocalyptic and mystical doctrines were never entirely lost from Orthodox Judaism, though their existence was at most times either denied or only grudgingly conceded.

all the prophetic writings: it could not be otherwise, given the nature of the beliefs they were upholding, the assemblages of historical documents which were available in common to them, and the fact that the later prophets were clearly cognizant of the writings of their predecessors. First, they all believed there would be a catastrophic *worsening* of the situation in which the people found itself. Then a time of ultimate crisis—"the day of the Lord"—when Yahweh would bring about, amid universal suffering, the utter humiliation and destruction of the sinners within Israel and of all Israel's external enemies: kings, empires, armies, pandemoniums of odious and worthless gods. Then the glorious triumph of "the saving remnant," who would (in the earlier writings) resume a free and peaceful life in their land, or (in the later writings) be led miraculously back from exile in order to take up their lives as a free people once again. Then a golden age, stretching indefinitely into the future: one which would see Yahweh's covenant renewed unbreakably with his people, who would never again stray from him or from his Law. Not only would the spirit of the people be changed, but the land itself, their inheritance under the covenant, and all the creatures in it, would be transformed, too. Only what was peaceful, fertile, long-lived, and gracious would be seen in it; justice alone would determine the relationships between men.

As for the nations around, their fate would be to remain in a state of perpetual subordination to Israel and the God of Israel. In a few passages—far fewer in relation to the bulk of the writing than both Jewish and Christian propagandists would generally have us believe—the nations would benefit from the new dispensation: out of it they would get peace, law, a discharge from the service of the contemptible gods they used to worship. (In Israel, or by Israel, as both Isaiah and the Book of Genesis put it, the nations of the world would "bless themselves.") More often, their condition is envisaged by the prophets essentially as one of servitude: Yahweh having exacted a full and bloody retribution from them for their past misdeeds, they would acknowledge their inferior status ("lick the dust"); they would pay tribute; they would live in awe and fear before Yahweh and his people. In other cases, again, the writings suggest a political and spiritual condition that lies indeterminately between the two possibilities outlined above, and that partakes (however illogically) of both.

But in no case that I am aware of in the prophetic writings, not even in those which seem most generous to the former enemies of Israel, is there any suggestion that the Israelites will merge with them, or will lose their special status as the people closest to God. On the contrary: the dream of renewal is a dream of the chosenness of the Israelites being not merely reconfirmed in private, as it were, between the two parties to the transaction, but made plain forever in its significance to all the peoples on earth; so plain that the best of them would be moved to admiration ("[They] will say this . . . is a wise and understanding people"— Deuteronomy 4:7), while the worst of them would never again dare lift a finger against the "kingdom of priests" whom God had chosen for his service.

We have seen that the very idea of the chosenness of Israel must always have carried with it the imputation of quasi-universal or at least supranational powers to Yahweh; otherwise he would not have been free to choose Israel among the nations. ("Now therefore if you will obey my voice and keep my covenant, you shall be my own possession among all peoples; *for all the earth is mine,* and you

shall be to me a kingdom of priests and a holy nation"—
Exodus 19:5–6.) It is also true, paradoxically perhaps, that
Yahweh's oneness, his solitariness as the protecting deity
of the Israelites, and of the Israelites alone, was in itself
bound to produce a "universalizing" of the powers imputed
to him. With whom could he share his powers? Surely not
with those contemptible foreign gods—not indefinitely, at
any rate. How could his worshipers do him honor but by
extending further and further the reach of his domains?
How could he help them if they did not? The worse things
got for the Israelites in their dealings with the successive
empires of the day, the more insistent and urgent was the
compulsion felt by the biblical writers to ascribe a truly
worldwide power to their God, so that he could put everything right once again. ("Universalism," Max Weber writes
brusquely and rather too simply in *The Sociology of Religion*, "was a product of international politics.")

But at every stage of the story the imputation of universality to God was seen as a way of *asserting* the uniqueness
and supremacy of Israel, never as a way of diminishing it,
or of abrogating it, or of looking forward to its supersession
by some more "advanced" state of equality among the nations whose destiny was believed to lie in his hands.

This seems to be the case even (and sometimes especially)
when the "conversion" of the nations to the worship of
Yahweh is spoken of; or when God expressly promises, as
he does in a series of prophecies which appear in Jeremiah
46–49, "to restore the fortunes" of the nations which had
been warring against the Israelites, after he has meted out
to them the punishments they deserve. For instance, in
reading the following passage from the Second Isaiah, which
contains perhaps the most explicit formulation to be found
in the entire Hebrew Scriptures of the idea of an active

"mission to the Gentiles,"* one cannot but be struck by
how "Israel-centric," if not outrightly "supremacist," it is
in spirit. (One notes also, incidentally, the characteristic
manner in which the fate of the individual, the servant
or prophet, mirrors or mimes exactly the fate of the people;
so much so that it is virtually impossible to distinguish
between them.)

> And now the Lord says,
> who formed me from the womb to be his servant,
> to bring Jacob back to him,
> and that Israel might be gathered to him,
> for I am honored in the eyes of the Lord,
> and my God has become my strength—
> he says:
> 'It is too light a thing that you should be my servant
> to raise up the tribes of Jacob
> and to restore the preserved of Israel;
> I will give you as a light to the nations,
> that my salvation may reach to the end of the earth."
> Thus says the Lord,
> the Redeemer of Israel and his Holy One,
> to one deeply despised, abhorred by the nations,
> the servant of rulers:
> 'Kings shall see and arise;
> princes, and they shall prostrate themselves;
> because of the Lord, who is faithful,
> the Holy One of Israel, who has chosen you.'
> Thus says the Lord:
> 'In a time of favor I have answered you,
> in a day of salvation I have helped you;
> I have kept you and given you
> as a covenant to the people,
> to establish the land,
> to apportion the desolate heritages;

---

* The instruction to Jonah to go to the "great city" of Nineveh "and cry against
it" is hardly a comparable case.

> saying to the prisoners, "Come forth,"
> to those who are in darkness, "Appear." '
>
> 49:5–9

Much the same can be said about the spirit of an even more frequently quoted "universalist" passage, from Isaiah 2:

> It shall come to pass in the latter days
> that the mountain of the house of the Lord
> shall be established as the highest of the mountains,
> and shall be raised above the hills;
> and all the nations shall flow to it,
> and many people shall come, and say:
> 'Come, let us go up to the mountain of the Lord,
> to the house of the God of Jacob;
> that he may teach us his ways
> and that we may walk in his paths.'
> For out of Zion shall go forth the law,
> and the word of the Lord from Jerusalem.
> He shall judge between the nations,
> and shall decide for many peoples;
> and they shall beat their swords into plowshares,
> and their spears into pruning hooks;
> nation shall not lift up sword against nation,
> neither shall they learn war any more.
>
> 2–4

Here, too, one detects the note of Israelite triumphalism which rings out so loudly elsewhere in First and Second Isaiah and in the other prophets. How could it be otherwise, given the inexpugnable association in the writers' minds between God, land, people, and sovereignty? The references to his teaching many peoples his laws, and to his judging between them, doubtless should be read as a manifestation of concern on his part for their welfare. But the language of the passage, as well as its immediate and overall contexts, forbid one to read it *only* in that sense. Clearly the prophet is here speaking also of the "political" condition of the people of Israel, relative to the nations who are to be taught and judged; as well as of what might be called the constitutional position of God as absolute and ultimate ruler within the Israelite polity. Lest we miss the point, we are told in an editorial note in verse 1 that the entire prophecy "concern[s] Judah and Jerusalem." (How secondary all those other peoples are!) The spiritual domination of Yahweh and the physical domination of his land over all others are inextricably linked, as the images used by the writer make clear ("the highest of the mountains"); the benefits accruing to others are wholly consequential upon the restoration of Jerusalem as the house of God; that restoration could never take place if his people, too, had not been restored to the whole of their inheritance—and more.

Several other points are relevant in considering these aspects of the passage. The word "flow" (Hebrew *nahar*) which is used by Isaiah in connection with the movement of foreign nations—uphill!—is also used by Jeremiah, in a context which is unmistakably one of spiritual-political enslavement.* The appearance in the Book of Micah (4:2–4) of these very verses from Isaiah was thought by the collators and redactors to be compatible with the most uncompromisingly exclusive of messages: "For all the peoples walk each in the name of its god, but we will walk in the name of the Lord our God for ever and ever." Indeed, immediately subsequent to the passage in Isaiah there is another, in which "the house of Jacob" is fiercely rebuked not only for admitting into its midst "divines from the East" and "soothsayers like the Philistines," but also for "striking

---

* And I will punish Bel in Babylon,
    and take out of his mouth what he has swallowed.
The nations shall no longer flow to him;
    the wall of Babylon has fallen.

JEREMIAH 51:44

hands with foreigners"—i.e., making friends with them. Needless to say, that passage is referred to far less often than the one which precedes it. To say that the one or the other passage is an "interpolation" may be true; it may also be not true: either way it hardly affects the argument.

According to Yehezkel Kaufmann's *The Religion of Israel*, there is only *one* instance in the entire Hebrew Scriptures of foreign peoples being referred to by Yahweh as "mine." This is really remarkable, when you consider the length of the Scriptures, and how often and emphatically within them Yahweh is said to be the creator and arbiter of everything on earth. The text in question is Isaiah 12:24; the peoples referred to are the Egyptians and the Assyrians. By contrast, there are literally innumerable passages which can be compared directly with this one from Micah in which—and it is a point of central significance—the universality of God's power is indistinguishable from and indispensable to the writer's fantasy of revenge:

> The nations shall see and be ashamed of all their might;
> they shall lay their hands on their mouths;
> their ears shall be deaf;
> they shall lick the dust like a serpent,
> like the crawling things of the earth;
> they shall come trembling out of their strongholds,
> they shall turn in dread to the Lord our God,
> and they shall fear because of thee.
>
> 7:16–17

The prospects of world domination (under Yahweh) which are held out to the Israelites by the prophets have long been an embarrassment to Jewish apologists, who have been anxious to underplay these aspects of the prophetic message, and to stress by contrast everything that might seem more easily digestible by other nations. Thus we are told much of the ethical and moral passions of the prophets, their concern for social justice and their hatred of meaningless, lip-service piety, and we hear rather less of the fiercely particularistic context in which these sentiments are lodged. We are also told that the chosenness of the Israelites was (or became, in the course of biblical and post-biblical history) a purely spiritual and exemplary vocation. As far as the Scriptures are concerned, this does not seem to me a sustainable claim: even allowing for the fact that one can perhaps see the dawning there of a "mission" or "witness" theology; and allowing, too, for a further handful of much-quoted utterances of an "ecumenical" kind to be found in post-exilic prophets like Zephaniah and Zechariah.

> Yea, at that time I will change the speech of the peoples
> to a pure speech,
> that all of them may call on the name of the Lord
> and serve him with one accord.
>
> ZEPHANIAH 3:9

Christian writers naturally seized upon such utterances precisely in order to wrest the God from his excessive and embarrassing preoccupation (from their point of view) with the fate of Israel. However, all these passages should be read in relation not only to the sheer bulk of the surrounding writings, but also to the momentum and direction of the narrative as a whole. To do this is to realize once again that the tension or contradiction in the Hebrew Scriptures between Yahweh the God of Israel, on the one hand, and Yahweh the creator of the universe and the governor of all mankind, on the other hand, is not really capable of a resolution which would simultaneously be true to the text and satisfy a demand for logical coherence. It has long been acknowledged that in this respect as in any other, a search for theoretical or doctrinal coherence is misguided. What the text offers instead are actions and passions which are linked both retrospectively and prospectively, and which reveal more and more about each other as the story of Israel and its God unfolds through time.

In the last chapter we looked at the violence with which the prophets and the historians attacked their own people, whom they held to be responsible for the calamities that had fallen upon them. I suggested there that some of this violence was a recoil from the writers' powerlessness in the face of their conquerors: *faute de mieux*, they turned on a weak and available target. But that very recoil would generate in its turn a surcharge of the rage and bitterness against the real or "objective" enemies of Israel. If, for their God's sake, they had not spared their own people, why should they spare those aliens? If *he*, the God of Israel, had not spared his own people for their sins, was he not now positively under an obligation to chastise the strangers in double and treble measure?

Such movements of mind and emotion are never one-way affairs. They feed off each other; they reinforce each other; they reward each other for the pains they inflict, and inflict pain on each other for the sake of the rewards and relief to come.

CHAPTER EIGHT

RENEWAL (Continued)

Any cunningly constructed narrative produces in its readers a feeling of "inevitability," which is often enough composed of two apparently contradictory elements. On the one hand, the reader is surprised at the way the narrative has developed; on the other, he feels that it has fulfilled his expectations. Many of the deepest expectations which a well-constructed story fulfills, in other words, are those which the reader did not consciously realize it had roused in him. He is satisfied in being taken aback, and taken aback by his own satisfaction. Because he sees in a new light everything that happened earlier in the story, he also imagines he can now see more clearly everything that lies ahead.

All this is relevant to an essential feature of the ecstatic and desperate promises of redemption which the prophets held out to successive generations of their people. In the act of looking forward to the grand denouement of the story—to the almost unimaginable transformations that land and people alike would undergo after the "day of the Lord"—they hark back in strikingly dramatic fashion to the beginning of the story. They do this by drawing a parallel between the tribulations of their own generations, and the sufferings of the people of Israel during the period of enslavement in Egypt and their subsequent wanderings through "the great and terrible wilderness." In effect, the prophets tell the people: "What we are experiencing now we have experienced in a different way before. The Lord saved us then. That is why we know he will do it again." All that had in the earlier record been presented as an account of literal fact now becomes an analogy, a metaphor, a precedent; and thus it becomes an inspiration, too.

Every effective national-historical myth is ultimately dependent upon the crystallization in a similar way of mere "events" into metaphors. This particular instance—the metaphorical transformation in the Scriptures of the period of slavery in Egypt, and the wanderings of Israel in the wilderness—has in its turn been used as a metaphor for their own condition by countless other groups, from Boers in South Africa to blacks in America. It is not difficult to see why. Anyone reading through the Scriptures must be moved by the way in which, in the hands of the prophets, and at a time of renewed national tribulation, the narrative suddenly coils back upon itself: as an increment, as it were, in the great power of the story originally told in Exodus. Nothing could indicate more clearly than this invocation of the past that the narrative was *one* for all those who composed it. Irrespective of the centuries that divided them, and irrespective of the nature of his own particular contribution, each writer knew that he was engaged in the same collective (and corrective) task as his forebears.

As usual, a few illustrations of the "Egyptian parallel" will have to stand in for many others. The entire book of Deuteronomy could be cited as a case in point here. Purporting to be the last testament of Moses to the Israelites before their entry into the promised land, it was in fact promulgated many hundreds of years after that event; it is thus an example of how an early phase of the history of the people could be used for elaborately exhortatory purposes at a time of acute national crisis. However, this "forgery," as Nietzsche bluntly called it in *The Anti-Christ*, is not the same thing as the deliberate and explicit use of historical analogy which I have in mind here. The paradoxical effect of these reminders of the past is at one and the same time to make Israel's history seem cyclical and *therefore* redemptive. Take, for example, the First Isaiah's imprecation against the Assyrians, and the promise that accompanies it:

> Therefore thus says the Lord, the Lord of hosts: 'O my people, who dwell in Zion, be not afraid of the Assyrians when they smite with the rod and lift up their staff against you as the Egyptians did. For in a very little while my indignation will come to an end, and my anger will be directed to their destruction. And the Lord of hosts will wield against them a scourge, as when he smote Midian at the rock of Oreb; and his rod will be over the sea, and he will lift it as he did in Egypt. And in that day his burden will depart from your shoulder, and his yoke will be destroyed from your neck.'
>
> 10:24–27

Or Jeremiah's promise in relation to a later set of conquerors and yet another land of bondage:

> Therefore, behold, the days are coming, says the Lord, when men shall no longer say, 'As the Lord lives who brought up the people of Israel out of the land of Egypt,' but 'As the Lord lives who brought up and led the descendants of the house of Israel out of the north country and out of all the countries where he had driven them.' Then they shall dwell in their own land.
>
> 23:7–8

The Second Isaiah also describes in detail how the past is to be gloriously reenacted:

> Go forth from Babylon, flee from Chaldea,
> declare this with a shout of joy, proclaim it,
> send it forth to the end of the earth;
> say, 'The Lord has redeemed his servant Jacob!'
>
> They thirsted not when he led them through the
>   deserts;
> he made water flow for them from the rock;
> he cleft the rock and the water gushed out.
>
> 48:20–21

Strangely enough, given the manner in which it is usually invoked, there are also instances in which a prophet looks back to the sojourn in the wilderness with an unmistakable degree of nostalgia. Hosea argues that because it was a time of greater simplicity and poverty than the subsequent period of settlement, it must also have been a period of greater moral purity. After comparing "Ephraim" (the northern kingdom) to a most sophisticated or citified kind of crook—a trader "in whose hands are false balances"—Hosea has Yahweh go on to proclaim:

> I am the Lord your God from the land of Egypt;
> I will again make you dwell in tents,
> as in the days of the appointed feast.
>
> . . . .
>
> It was I who knew you in the wilderness,
> in the land of drought;
> but when they had fed to the full,
> they were filled, and their heart was lifted up;
> therefore they forgot me.
>
> 12:9; 13:5–6

The narrative cunning which I have ascribed to some of the prophets was seen very differently by them. They ascribed it to Yahweh. It may be objected that they ascribed everything to Yahweh;* why, then, should special mention be made of the fact here? Well, the point I want to emphasize is that the prophets actually saw this second redemption in quasi-literary or critical terms rather like those I have just used. They had come to regard Yahweh's actions as elements in an *overall* "plot" or design which, like some master dramatist or storyteller, he was unfolding at his own pace, and in his own surprising yet mysteriously satisfying way, with the intention of finally overwhelming and stupefying his audience. Because the history they were transcribing or commenting upon was leading irresistibly to a great climax or denouement, the prophets themselves began to see all the windings and reversals and (especially) the repetitions within the course of the narrative as having been designed by Yahweh precisely for the sake of their ultimate dramatic effect.

> The Lord of hosts has sworn:
> 'As I have planned,
> so shall it be,
> and as I have purposed,
> so shall it stand.'

ISAIAH 14:24

> Have you not heard
> that I determined it long ago?
> I planned from days of old
> what now I bring to pass,

---

* It is extraordinary how often one finds, in every possible context, the name of Yahweh coupled directly with a verb describing some dynamic, wholly self-motivated and decisive action. A sample list of these verbs, drawn from the Revised Standard Version in a couple of minutes, reads alphabetically: appoint, arise, avenge, bind, bring, change, deal with, destroy, dispossess, drive out, enter (into a place or a judgment), establish, forget, gather, give, guide, help, hew, judge, keep, know, love, lead, make (a thing, an end, a covenant), pity, pluck down, punish, reject, remember, renew, repair, restore, send, set up, show, spare, stir, take (pity or vengeance), uncover, vanquish, watch, waste. . . .

that you should make fortified cities
crash into heaps of ruins,
while their inhabitants, shorn of strength,
are dismayed and confounded.

ISAIAH 37:26–27

Now many nations
are assembled against you,
saying, 'Let her be profaned,
and let our eyes gaze upon Zion.'
But they do not know
the thoughts of the Lord,
they do not understand his plan,
that he has gathered them as
sheaves to the threshing floor.

MICAH 4:11–12

To believe that history tells or is going to tell a story of this kind is to believe also that its course is foreordained. You cannot have the one without the other. For if history is the unfolding of a predetermined plan, then its end must always in some sense have been "there," waiting for its moment to arrive. The prophets never articulated this belief or presupposition; but the force and clarity with which they expressed it have had an incalculable effect on historical thinking subsequently. When one considers all the plots or great schemes which history has since been said to be unfolding, for the unutterable benefit of this or that group, and the final ruin of others, one is tempted to say that this particular scriptural legacy has been of even greater significance than the idea of the chosen people. But the distinction between these two ideas—that of the chosen people, on the one hand, and that of history-as-plot, on the other—is impossible to maintain. The need for the history of the people to move in a foreordained direction arose directly from the obligation which was placed upon God to make his choice evident to all. (In later, secularized versions of the tale, history itself virtually becomes the god: it is the irresistible yet impersonal force which has somehow "planned from days of old" what it is sooner or later going to bring to pass.) The God who was able to discharge his obligations by leading the Israelites into the promised land from the south had a much simpler task than the one who, almost a thousand years later, was engaged by his devout followers to secure their reentry into it from the north, in the teeth of all conceivable odds. The prophecies of renewal must be considered, among other things, as a direct challenge to Yahweh to justify retrospectively the tribulations he had visited upon his people. But then, the higher the stakes, and the bigger the entire field over which the game was played, the greater his prowess.

The pattern we have seen throughout is once again quite clear. Just as the defeat and exile of the chosen people were used as unassailable proof of God's moral intensity and power, so, in the eyes of the prophets, defeat and exile made the history of their people virtually identical with the history of the whole world. Their God's obligation to make manifest his choice to all the far-flung nations was, so to speak, his biggest opportunity yet.

Much of the great work of national renewal and restoration was to be accomplished, as everyone knows, through the agency of a specially chosen and divinely endowed individual, "the Lord's anointed," the Messiah. The development of this idea from its fairly modest and "empirical" beginnings in some of the prophecies of the First Isaiah, where the prophet is usually taken to have been speaking of his hopes for the reign of King Hezekiah of Judah, to the adumbration of obscurely apocalyptic figures like the

Son of Man in Daniel and subsequent writings, including the Gospels—all this is a specialist topic which must be left to the specialists. The relevant point here is that for the prophets who wrote of him in idealized yet recognizably human terms, the redeemer was exactly what his title and lineage as "a shoot of David" indicated: he was to be the king of Judah, its political-religious leader, under Yahweh.

Hence both pre-exilic and post-exilic prophets were able to hail real personages, particular individuals whose prospects seemed especially promising to them, as the one whose coming had long been foretold. The case of Hezekiah, who ruled over Judah from 726 to 697 B.C., has just been mentioned; scholars also believe that much later prophecies in Haggai and Malachi speak in comparable terms of the post-exilic leader Zerubbabel. In the last chapter I said that the prophets recorded "events" which had not yet happened; and that they did this precisely in order to make those very events occur. That description applies also to passages written out of the conviction that the future so long dreamed of had actually arrived at last, or was on the very point of doing so.

The most dramatic of all the messianic moments recorded in the Scriptures occurred when King Cyrus of Persia, after his victory over the Babylonians, encouraged the exiles to return to their land: an event which produced passages of unparalleled wonder and triumph.

> But now thus says the Lord,
> he who created you, O Jacob,
> he who formed you, O Israel:
> 'Fear not, for I have redeemed you;
> I have called you by name, you are mine.
> When you pass through the waters I will be with you;

and through the rivers, they shall not overwhelm you;
when you walk through fire you shall not be burned,
and the flame shall not consume you.
For I am the Lord your God,
the Holy One of Israel, your Saviour.
I give Egypt as your ransom,
Ethiopia and Seba in exchange for you.
Because you are precious in my eyes,
and honoured, and I love you,
I give men in return for you,
peoples in exchange for your life.
Fear not, for I am with you;
I will bring your offspring from the east.
and from the west I will gather you;
I will say to the north, Give up,
and to the south, Do not withhold;
bring my sons from afar
and my daughters from the end of the earth. . . . .

ISAIAH 43:1–6

Sing, O heavens, for the Lord has done it;
shout, O depths of the earth;
break forth into singing, O mountains,
O forest, and every tree in it!
For the Lord has redeemed Jacob,
and will be glorified in Israel.

Thus says the Lord, your Redeemer,
who formed you from the womb:
. . . .
who confirms the word of his servant,
and performs the counsel of his messengers;
who says of Jerusalem, 'She shall be inhabited,'
and of the cities of Judah, 'They shall be built,
and I will raise up their ruins';
who says to the deep, 'Be dry,
I will dry up your rivers';
who says of Cyrus, 'He is my shepherd,

> and he shall fulfil all my purpose';
> saying of Jerusalem, 'She shall be built,'
> and of the temple, 'Your foundation shall be laid.'
>
> ISAIAH 44:23–24, 26–28

These particular prophecies from Second Isaiah in fact make no mention of any individual or personal Messiah for Israel: it is characteristic of the confusion surrounding such subjects that the only reference within this set of poems to "the anointed of the Lord" is to Cyrus himself (45:1). In several ways the references to Cyrus in Isaiah 45 illustrate beautifully the tensions between the universal powers ascribed to Yahweh, and his special and overriding preoccupation with the fate of Israel. In the opening verses of the chapter, God speaks directly to Cyrus, and "calls him by name," and promises great conquests and treasures to him, and repeatedly informs him that there is no God other than Yahweh himself, "from the rising of the sun to the west." At the same time, lest Cyrus should get ideas above even his exalted station, God is at pains twice to tell him that "you do not know me"; and that everything promised to him is "for the sake of my servant Jacob and Israel my chosen."

Anyway, expectations pitched so high were bound to be disappointed. This was true not only of those prophecies about the conditions that would prevail upon the return from Babylon—prophecies which turned out to be very wide of the mark—but of all the exaggeratedly hopeful declarations in the prophetic books about the great times ahead for Israel, whether or not these were attached explicitly to specific historic events. Common sense would suggest that the more precisely the coming of the Messiah and the messianic age was foretold, the more damaging to the community of believers would be the subsequent disappointment. But common sense turns out to be an unreliable guide in such matters. Because prophetic hopes and expectations had always so greatly outrun events—any possible events— what happened was that the writers in the later apocalyptic tradition began to expect utterly fantastic and outrightly impossible events; to imagine not redeemed or reformed worlds poignantly resembling our own, but wholly new worlds. "Then I saw a new heaven and a new earth, for the first heaven and the first earth had passed away, and the sea was no more. And I saw the holy city, the new Jerusalem, coming down out of heaven from God, prepared as a bride for her husband" (Revelation 21:1–2).

In thinking about the future redemption, in whatever terms it was conceived, one simple yet far-reaching question troubled some of the prophets. Who was to enjoy the golden time ahead? Who exactly was to be redeemed? For the most part they were content to answer: The people of Israel as a whole. It was for them that Yahweh was storing up his blessings at the end of days. But they did not always find this answer wholly satisfying. After all, they themselves had described graphically the destruction that had already been, or was shortly to be, wreaked upon Israel in retribution for its sins: heaps of corpses in the streets; burning buildings; violated and enslaved women; columns of prisoners led into exile; famine, disease, cannibalism. Who would be left, after this savage cleansing? What instrument would be available to Yahweh to carry out his great work of restoration?

Hence the concept of the "remnant." In some cases this word, and words of similar purport, appear to have been used neutrally: simply as a reference to those who survived. For example, we find in Micah (2:12): "I will gather the remnant of Israel like sheep in a fold," or in Isaiah (10:21):

"A remnant will return, the remnant of Jacob, to the mighty God." Even the elaborate quasi-Homeric or Virgilian simile in the quotation below seems to imply a more or less random process of selection or survival:

> And it shall be as when the reaper gathers standing
>   grain
> and his arm harvests the ears,
> and as when one gleans the ears of grain
> in the Valley of Rephaim.
> Gleanings will be left in it,
> as when an olive tree is beaten—
> two or three berries
> in the top of the highest bough,
> four or five
> on the branches of a fruit tree,
> says the Lord God of Israel.
>
> ISAIAH 17:5–6

Not to speak of this one used by Amos!

> Thus says the Lord: 'As the shepherd rescues from the mouth of the lion two legs, or a piece of an ear, so shall the people of Israel who dwell in Samaria be rescued, with the corner of a couch and part of a bed.'
>
> 3:12

However, when Jeremiah uses a more or less comparable metaphor, we are not left in any doubt about the moral intention behind the selection:

> Go up through her vine-rows and destroy,
> but make not a full end;
> strip away her branches,
> for they are not the Lord's.
>
> 5:10

In other words, the vine-rows that are *not* destroyed must be assumed to be the Lord's: worth saving for their merits.

They are, to put it starkly, chosen: the chosen few within what was supposedly a chosen people overall. They represent the true Israel, the real Israel, garnered by Yahweh out of the mass that had shown itself to be unworthy of him.

The idea of the remnant in this "stronger" sense of the word—which should include not only those who had always remained faithful to Yahweh, but also those who were truly penitent after their chastisement at his hands—is found in virtually all the prophetic books, of both the pre-exilic and the post-exilic periods (Micah, First and Second Isaiah, Jeremiah, Zephaniah, Zechariah, etc.). One can guess that at all times during the historical periods covered by the texts, particular groups must have cherished among themselves the belief that they were in fact more chosen than others among the chosen people. To know how widely these beliefs did eventually spread, and how influential they could become, one has to look at the apocalyptic literature, and the writings of the Qumran sect, and the histories of Josephus; not to speak of the Gospels themselves. In all these one finds sects which believe passionately that they represent the worthy remnant of which the prophetic literature of their ancestors had spoken: a small, truly chosen group surviving precariously but decisively within a counterfeit Israel, a nation composed of sinful leaders, evil priests, and misled masses.

The paradoxical conclusion that can be drawn from this is that the very concept of chosenness is inherently fissiparous. Or to put it another way: the conviction among the members of a group that they have been divinely chosen to serve some special, trans-historical end will help to hold them together—until they fall apart into so many internecine factions.

CHAPTER NINE

PROPHETS, POETS,
AND POLITICIANS

"The story of the stories" in the Hebrew Scriptures goes no further than the point reached in the last two chapters. Beginning with the entry of the people into the land promised them by their God, it virtually ends with the visions offered at different times by the prophets of God once more restored to sovereignty, and his people to independence and preeminence. With these visions, as many writers have remarked, the narrative concludes its great circular movement. It has seen the people move from a condition of homeless nomadism to possession of the land; from possession of the land to dispossession from it; from dispossession to exile; from exile to the hope or vision, at least, of reentry and true repossession. Or one might say that the narrative has moved from describing enslavement to liberation; from liberation to enslavement; and from enslavement to liberation once more—again, in the case of the last, as an imaginative assertion or demand, rather than as an accomplished fact.

But can such a story ever really come to an end? Can the circular movement which the story has described be convincingly brought to a halt? The prophets certainly willed that it should; hence their great, final effort of the imagination, in presenting the renewal-to-come as a state of eternal rest, or arrest.

Against that feat the "material" facts of history have in some ways been of remarkably little avail. The kingdom was never restored as the prophets had dreamed of it; not surprisingly, in view of the fact that their diagnosis of why it went under can appear plausible only to a biblical fundamentalist. The bald fact is that Samaria and Judea were crushed because they were subject to ceaseless attack from the empires to the north and south, each of which sought to control the sole overland route through which the other could threaten it. Given the terrain occupied by the Hebrew kingdoms, it is impossible to imagine them surviving as independent political entities for much longer than they did: irrespective, that is, of whom their population worshiped or of how well they behaved to one another. What has to be taken into account, therefore, is that the biblical story was able to act as it has on men's lives for centuries and millennia precisely because its *untruth* appealed to their imaginations at a depth the facts could never reach.

It is an untruth of a quite special kind, of course. The appeal of the story becomes comprehensible only if one has a sufficiently high regard for the passionate and literal conviction with which the prophets put forward the narrative of Yahweh's will as an explanation of the history in which they saw their people entrapped. (Or, one might say, the historical narrative through which they explained his will.) They did literally believe that the Assyrians and Babylonians were nothing more than Yahweh's instruments for the chastisement of Israel; they did literally believe that these chastisements were being visited on the people because of their sins; they did literally believe he would turn his wrath from them if they repented. Now, so far from this element in their work being secondary or inconsequential, one which is separable from its literary power and moral zeal, something perhaps to be shuffled away as an embarrassment or irrelevance, I have argued throughout that it is the essential condition of their poetic and moral vision; its very source and heart. They had the imaginative audacity to mean everything they said; they embraced *à outrance* the historical facts as they perceived them; *hence* the unparalleled power of their poetry. The ruthlessness and consistency with which the prophets extended the myth of God's choice, his gift to his chosen people, and his anger at them for their disobedience and immorality, together with the amazing promises for the future they managed to wring out of this story, enabled it to generate new religions, new moral codes, and new types or models of human behavior.

To this day—and I deliberately take my example from a secular area of contemporary life—one can discern the Scriptures, among other influences, lurking behind a common, solemn notion of the role of the writer in society. According to this notion, he has a special capacity to diagnose the innermost moral evils and failures of civilization, and to warn us of the disasters that these will bring in their train, unless we attend to him and mend our ways. I wonder how many of those who assume this role—poets, novelists, playwrights, critics, and other such self-appointed inspectors-general of entire cultures and phases of civilization—care to remember one disconcerting fact about the utterances of their biblical predecessors: namely, that the Hebrew kingdoms did not collapse for the reasons the prophets had proclaimed. To be bald about it again, historically speaking: the societies that developed along the banks of great rivers like the Nile and the Tigris-Euphrates were bound to be more powerful and hence more expansive than any that managed to perch itself among the rocky hillsides and exiguous valleys of Judea and Samaria. The rest—the "facts" of conquest and enslavement—duly followed.

Only, the Hebrews had a story to tell; their conquerors did not. That was the sole advantage they had over them. And what an advantage that has turned out to be, all said and done! *Toutes proportions gardées,* something similar might perhaps be said about the myths adumbrated by some of the great modern writers. Their diagnoses of the ailments of our civilization, and the causes and cures they propose for these ills, may all be quite wide of the mark. Probably they are. The fact that they are believed to be accurate, however, does give them an objective importance which it would be pointless to deny.

To say that the prophets were "mistaken" in their diagnosis of the fate of the Israelite kingdoms, and that it was the power of the myth which secured the survival of their message as a whole, is to oversimplify matters in at least two important respects. The first is that much of what the prophets wrote was not in fact "wrong" about the Israelite kingdoms; it could not have been wrong, because what they said would apply in greater or lesser degree to any kingdom or polity the world has known. They are all places of injustice and institutionalized cruelty; and the prophets were crying out against the one they knew for being so. Pleas for justice and charity in dealings between men and their neighbors, or between men and the state, can never be out of season.

Secondly, as I have already indicated, their writing survived because the myth infused itself into, and indeed largely generated, the specifically literary and metaphoric power with which they expressed themselves.

It is difficult to say anything that would be both brief and to the point about these aspects of their writings. Still, I shall try. With regard to the first, scholars all seem to agree that the insistence of the prophets upon the "primacy of morality," rather than ritual, in the relationship between a man and his God was unprecedented in Israel and outside it. Their conviction that only those who were righteous in their behavior to their fellow men could truly do honor to God, and win his favor, since he himself was wholly righteous, is thus represented as a great moral advance in the history of mankind. Because Yahweh was a God of righteousness, Amos, Micah, Isaiah, and Jeremiah have him express disgust with formal sacrifice and lip service: "Your new moons and your appointed feasts my soul hates; they have become a burden to me" (Isaiah 1:14). For this reason Isaiah cries woe to those exploiters and expropriators among his countrymen who "add field to field until there is no room," and woe again to those who "decree iniquitous decrees . . . and keep writing oppression, to turn aside the needy from justice" (5:8; 10:1–2); for this reason Micah claimed that nothing more was asked of a man than "to do justice and to love kindness and to walk humbly with your God" (6:8).

But I repeat that the categorical or universal nature of the prophets' moral injunctions to their people should not lead us to imagine that they demanded or wished to express a dilution or diminution of national consciousness. The intended effect of their writings was actually to intensify that consciousness. To begin with, they brought a whole new category of wrongdoing—moral crimes—into the arena of what Yehezkel Kaufmann, in *The Religion of Israel*, calls "the crucial national sins": i.e., the sins for which the nation as a whole would be punished, and not merely the individuals who committed them. Sexual, political, and social wrongdoing had been forbidden in the lawbooks, too; but in those books only idolatry, it was said, would lead to the enslavement and expulsion of the people. The prophets did away with that distinction. At the same time, they insisted that their God would restore Israel to Jerusalem and grant it revenge on all its enemies precisely *because* he was just and righteous. After all that Israel had suffered (and at his hands!), it was the least he could do. Being just and righteous, he would one day acknowledge that he had punished his people sufficiently for the sins they had committed; thereupon he would turn the full force of his wrath on the enemies who were at present tormenting them and exulting in their humiliation.

That much is clear. That much must be said outright. Yet I would argue that this mode of presenting history is itself predicated on a sense of the unity of human experience which runs deeper than the writers wholly realized. For all that is apparently remorseless and mechanical about their vision of history as a dramatic series of reversals of fortune, which could come to an end in a dream world effectively outside or beyond time—or perhaps because of the remorseless and mechanical manner in which it operates—this vision actually cuts radically across the writers' conviction of the unique status of their people. (Much more so, I think, than the prophetic passages which ambiguously offer other nations selected blessings of the messianic age to come.) In certain unexpected, hidden ways, some of which have already been looked at, it questions the uniqueness of Israel, if only by demonstrating again how equivocal were the ways of its God. The weapon of vicissitude would never leave his hand. It was to be used against all peoples, his favorites not excluded.

Isolating the ethical teachings of the prophets from the overall myth is just as difficult as attempting to isolate the specifically literary or metaphorical qualities of their writing. The quotations from the prophetic books which have been scattered throughout these pages have, I hope, reminded readers of some of those qualities. It would be pointless to try to assemble an anthology or a catalogue of particular passages which seem to me especially powerful from a literary point of view; in any case, I am precluded from doing so by my dependence on translations, in which many crucial poetic effects are bound to be lost.* It is true that even in translation one can hear that the "noise" made by Jeremiah, say, is different from that made by Amos or First Isaiah: inevitably, given the differing temperaments and preoccupations of each of them. But there would not

---

*Because of its system of highly inflected, three-letter roots for most nouns and verbs, and because of the extreme degree of syntactic compression which this system permits, the Hebrew language lends itself readily to elaborate puns, repetitions, and rhetorical inversions of all kinds. Perhaps the most spectacular example I have come across, in my reading of a parallel Hebrew-English text, is the passage in Isaiah (24:17–20) which in the English of the Revised Standard Version reads:

> Terror, and the pit, and the snare
> are upon you, O inhabitants of the earth!
> He who flees at the sound of the terror
> shall fall into the pit;
> and he who climbs out of the pit
> shall be caught in the snare.
> For the windows of heaven are opened
> and the foundations of the earth tremble.
> The earth is utterly broken,
> the earth is rent asunder,
> the earth is violently shaken.
> The earth staggers like a drunken man,
> it sways like a hut.

In the original Hebrew the passage consists of an amazing concatenation of packed, repetitive chains of syllables, expressing a series of constantly shifting, reflexive meanings. The first line can be transliterated as

> *paḥad ve-paḥat ve-paḥ*

and as the verses begin, so they continue.

be much point, again, in my trying to convey a sense of the differences; other considerations aside, I am far more interested in what unites than in what divides them.

All that said, there are a few distinctively literary-critical remarks worth making here. (The famous poetic device of "parallelism" will be discussed in another context, in the next chapter.) The first is very general indeed. Any reader of the Scriptures will be struck by the contrast between the terseness and rapidity of the narrative books, and the extravagantly repetitious, tirelessly metaphorical exfoliations of the prophetic books. (The comparison is not as unfair as it may seem: the prophetic books are as much concerned as the narratives with the course of events in Israelite history, past and future. In any case, one finds repetition and downright incoherence in the narratives, too, as a result of the spatchcocking together of material from the different sources.) On this subject I can perhaps best speak autobiographically or anecdotally. When I was working on my novel *The Rape of Tamar*—a fictional retelling of the story about the rape of King David's only daughter by her brother, Amnon, and the revenge subsequently taken upon him by yet another brother, Absalom—it occurred to me that every phrase, virtually every word, in the relevant chapter of 2 Samuel was like a seed. Dry, hard, small, compressed, apparently lifeless, it was capable of astonishing growth, if it was planted in one's mind and saturated with whatever capacity one had for imaginative response and understanding. Reading almost any of the prophetic books is an experience of a greatly different kind. There are many concise, pregnant utterances within them: agreed. But the more one reads, the more one feels impelled to put up a defense against them—a kind of breakwater in the mind— to prevent oneself from being overwhelmed by the constant, unrelenting roar of verbiage, beating down upon the page with all the fury and ultimate monotony of waves on a beach.

The assiduity and ingenuity with which the prophets say the same things over and over again in slightly different ways produce one surprising side effect. One can get from their books a richly detailed picture of what conditions of daily life must have been like for the people of Israel during the monarchical period. The narratives tell us much; in many respects the prophets tell us even more. The persistent use they make of the most familiar objects and practices in their imagery is just one sign of their power as creative artists; especially when one thinks of the hortatory and minatory ends for which they wrote. From their books one can learn about the climate and topography of the country; about the crops people grew on their land; the clothes they wore;* the herds they tended; the furniture they had in their houses; the ways in which they stored their food; the occupations they followed; the kinds of medical treatment that were available to them; and much else besides.

Samuel Johnson would not have agreed with what I have just said about the appearance of familiar objects in great poetry. He found risible and disgusting Shakespeare's phrase "the blanket of the dark," in *Macbeth;* the vulgar associations of the word "blanket" were in Dr. Johnson's view incompatible with the dignity of high tragedy. One wonders what he might have made of Isaiah's vividly metaphoric

---

* "In that day the Lord will take away the finery of the anklets, the headbands, and the crescents; the pendants, the bracelets, and the scarfs; the headdresses, the armlets, the sashes, the perfume boxes, and the amulets; the signet rings and nose rings; the festal robes, the mantles, the cloaks, and the handbags; the garments of gauze, the linen garments, the turbans, and the veils" (ISAIAH 3:18–23).

In *Everyday Life in Old Testament Times*, E. W. Heaton warns us that "this formidable collection is intended as a deliberate caricature" of what was available in the way of feminine attire.

description of how little security or comfort the kingdom of Judah had gained in making an alliance with Egypt against the Assyrian invader. "For the bed is too short," he wrote, in evocation of everyone's memory of a tormented night, "to stretch oneself on it; and the covering too narrow to wrap oneself in it" (28:20).

But then, the prophets never cared about their dignity or grandeur, or the dignity and grandeur of their readers; only Yahweh's mattered to them. To illustrate the demands and admonitions of their God they were prepared not only to use the lowliest objects ("wash-pots," etc.) as metaphors in their writings; they were also ready to make, as it were, walking icons of themselves. They transformed themselves into visible personifications of the abject state and forlorn hopes of Israel. Isaiah went about barefoot and with loosened garments as a "sign and portent" of the disasters that would follow the alliance with Egypt referred to above; Jeremiah appeared with a yoke over his shoulders to show the Israelites that they had no choice but to submit to the Babylonians; Amos proclaimed his wife's infidelities as an analogue of Israel's infidelities to Yahweh; Ezekiel lay on his side for a number of days equal to the years that the people would suffer their punishment.

Synecdoche, metaphor, personification—these are terms used in rhetoric and literary criticism. Yet they can be properly invoked here to characterize not the writings of the prophets (as transcribed by them or by their disciples) but their reported actions. Nothing could illustrate better than these pieces of dramatic mimicry, these "real" yet wholly figurative actions, the ever-trembling, self-energizing *instability* of the relationship between the literal and the metaphorical in the Scriptures. Through their actions the prophets become a living sign of the people's true condition; just as the entire written record of the people's suffering and of its hopes of redemption was eventually to be seen by some interpreters as a parabolic prefiguring of the death and resurrection of one whom they believed to be greater than any of the prophets.

Elements from the prophetic writings were absorbed into Christian thought and doctrine in a multitude of ways and at many different levels; so many it is impossible to enumerate them. One recognizes the direct influence of the prophets in, for example, some of the most important "facts" about Jesus' life which are presented in the Gospels, especially in the Gospel of Matthew; in the justifications offered by Paul for many of his boldest theological assertions; in the frenzies of the revelations described by John of Patmos; in the different modes of messiahship which are imputed to Jesus. The emphasis the prophets placed on inner piety rather than cultic practices was interpreted as a foreshadowing of that liberation from the "yoke" of scriptural Law which Jesus was said to have delivered; the condemnation by the prophets of the Israelites could be used both as an explanation of why they had rejected their Savior (what else could be expected of so blind and corrupt a nation?) and as yet another compelling reason for the abandonment of their Law (look how little it had availed them when they had most needed to act rightly!). Moreover, the lives of the prophets were seen as a type of the life of Jesus, as Jesus himself is made to point out: "O Jerusalem, Jerusalem, killing the prophets and stoning those who are sent to you!" (Luke 13:34).

What might come as a surprise to the reader, however, is not that the prophets were killed and stoned; but that these "political demagogues and pamphleteers," as Max

Weber calls them in his *Ancient Judaism*, were actually given so much latitude in spreading their message. There is evidence of two kinds about the degree to which they enjoyed freedom of speech: the explicit evidence of the prophets' own descriptions of how they were able to go about the streets speaking to the populace, and to enter the palaces of kings and denounce them and their servants to their face; and the implicit evidence of the fact that their writings are available to us. The last point is a simple one; so simple it is almost always overlooked. For all that was seditious and denunciatory of the authorities and the populace about these discourses, they were nevertheless held in sufficient esteem to be collected and carefully preserved by the followers of the prophets in their own and succeeding generations. So far from being censored or destroyed, they were treasured by at least some of those to whom they were addressed.

This is not to deny the sufferings certain prophets went through at the hands of indignant kings and their officers. Amos was banished from the northern kingdom, we are told, and Jeremiah thrown into a dungeon, because of the offense they gave; in the records of the earlier, "nonwriting" prophets, in 1 Kings for example, there are instances of a similar fate falling upon Elijah and Micaiah. Legends like these, glorifying men who defied authority for Yahweh's sake, were a vital part of the tradition; as an incitement and justification, they lay behind the later prophets' conception of themselves and their duties. "Is it you, you troubler of Israel?" King Ahab says by way of greeting to Elijah, in Chapter 19 of 1 Kings; in the following chapter he greets the prophet more wearily still: "Have you found me, O my enemy?" One cannot imagine any other society of the ancient Near East producing a literature in which relations between kings and prophets would be dramatized in such terms; and in which all the sympathy of the writers would go toward the troubler of the king's peace.

The existence of such a powerful and long-standing tradition of dissent, enshrined within the sacred history of the nation, should in itself go some way toward modifying the uniformly black view of Israelite society which the prophets themselves presented. While the notion of historical causality held by the prophets positively compelled them to present such a picture of the society, we have to take into account the fact that that very society gave them the opportunity to go about their task of denunciation; and also, more remarkably still, that their denunciations became the "official" view which the society, under ever-increasing stress, began to hold of itself. (Which is not the same thing as saying, of course, that everyone or even most people believed it or acted on it.) "At last," states S. A. Cook, in *An Introduction to the Bible,* in a manner not untypical of a certain kind of pronouncement on the subject, "the prophets came to realize the hopeless rottenness of Israel . . ." How does he know of the hopeless rottenness of Israel? Because unlike most other peoples, the ancient Israelites took immense pains to tell him about it!

Tolerance of others was not, however, a virtue that the prophets themselves displayed. Those who disagreed with them on matters of practical policy, let alone on ethical, social, or cultic issues, they regarded simply as enemies of Yahweh and Israel, who acted and thought as they did because they were "evil." Never for any other reason. In other words, distinctions between different kinds of issues or modes of discourse simply did not exist for them. Even when the nature of the disagreements between prophet and court on political matters emerge most clearly, as they do in the books of First Isaiah and Jeremiah, both of whom obviously had sustained access to the highest councils of state, the opponents of the prophets are never granted the dignity of holding to their views out of honest conviction. Yet through the barrage of abuse directed by the prophets against their opponents one can make out the positions held by each side in the dispute. For example, the account of the relationship between Zedekiah the king and Jeremiah, during the last, desperate days of the monarchy, is as dramatic, and as full of compelling detail, as any other episode in the Scriptures. Jeremiah, the pessimist, the man who declares that there is no alternative to surrendering to the Babylonians, is accused by one faction in the court of "weakening the hands of the soldiers who are left in the city." Because the war party, the "hawks," are the stronger faction, he is cast into a cistern and left there to die; he is rescued from it by a servant of the king, who draws him out by ropes (carefully telling him beforehand to "put rags and clothes between your armpits and the ropes" so that he will not be hurt); then the king, who is afraid of his own courtiers, secretly consults the prophet . . . and all, as we know, to no avail.

To us, cloak-and-dagger activities of this kind may seem a far cry from a poet's practice of his craft, or even from the prophet's duties as a moral and religious mentor of his people. To the ancient Israelites, however, the roles of prophet, poet, and embattled political figure seem to have been indistinguishable from one another: indeed, the adoption of the one role necessarily demanded the adoption of the others. Political decisions either reflected the will of Yahweh or failed to do so; as the mouthpiece of Yahweh, the prophet had to let the people know which of these two paths had been taken; in so doing he naturally delivered his oracles in the form in which they would be most impressive and memorable to his listeners. That is, in the form of verse.

It should not be surprising, therefore, that even in the most terrifying of the prophetic forebodings and denunciations, one can recognize that irrepressible delight in the writer's own powers without which no memorable work of literature has ever been produced. Each prophet in his own way uses a variety of dramatic, rhetorical, and metaphorical effects of a consciously artistic kind. To remark on the elements of artistic self-delight in their work is not to detract from the seriousness of their intentions, or from their total commitment to the messages they wished to deliver. On the contrary: it is merely to remind ourselves what a complicated thing imaginative seriousness always is.

It is very difficult for us to look on the prophets in terms other than those which they themselves explicitly proposed. They insisted that all history had a meaning and a predetermined direction: it was making toward a great settling of accounts and a final act of national salvation. Inevitably, given the widespread influence that this kind of historical view has had, not least because of the manner in which the prophetic tradition was incorporated into Christianity, we are inclined to think of the prophets themselves as representing one stage in a more or less unilinear *advance*, morally and intellectually speaking, on everything that had gone before them. This tendency is made stronger by the undoubted fact that the prophets did develop and expand with great boldness the myth they had inherited: thus their writings do not only speak of an advance; they actually embody one.

However, there is another way of looking at their work.

As I have already suggested, the prospects of salvation which the prophets held out to the Israelites can be seen as just a further manifestation (on this occasion a longed-for manifestation) of the inexorable historical process which they themselves had shown to be Yahweh's way of revealing himself in the world. In the era of prophecy, Yahweh had brought disaster upon the Israelites, to the joy of their enemies, the Assyrians, the Babylonians, and others; earlier he had brought disaster upon the Canaanites, to the joy of the Israelites; earlier still he had abandoned the Israelites to enslavement under a pharaoh—a pharaoh whose horse and rider were eventually to be thrown into the sea, so that the women of Israel might sing and dance. . . .

In the following chapter I shall examine the most striking of the means by which the prophets summarized this entire narrative: a summary that takes the surprising and yet curiously appropriate form of a single, simple metaphor, or group of metaphors, which appears with almost obsessive frequency in their writings.

CHAPTER TEN

PERIPETEIA

The plot that has to be summarized is, after all, a very simple one. The exalted are brought low; the low and despised are exalted. The powerful are crushed; those who had been crushed are given power. The possessors are dispossessed; the dispossessed are given possession. The victims become the victors; the victors victims. The childless become fertile; those who have children lose them. The deaf hear and the blind see; the fat and proud go hungry and suffer the loss of their faculties.

Many of the most concise and most expressive summaries of the workings of this historical process are to be found in the prophecies of First and Second Isaiah and the Psalms. However, an idea of the range, persistence, and centrality of the texts embodying these ideas can be conveyed only by extensive quotation from many sources.

> Behold, the Lord, the Lord of hosts
> will lop the boughs with terrifying power;
> the great in height will be hewn down,
> and the lofty will be brought low.
>
> ISAIAH 10:33

> How you are fallen from heaven,
> O Day Star, son of Dawn!

How you are cut down to the ground,
you who laid the nations low!

ISAIAH 14:12

For he has brought low
the inhabitants of the height, the lofty city.
He lays it low, lays it low to the ground,
casts it to the dust.
The foot tramples it,
the feet of the poor,
the steps of the needy.

ISAIAH 26:5–6

In that day the deaf shall hear
the words of a book,
and out of their gloom and darkness
the eyes of the blind shall see.

ISAIAH 29:18

Every valley shall be lifted up,
and every mountain and hill be made low;
the uneven ground shall become level,
and the rough places a plain.

ISAIAH 40:4

Now therefore hear this, you lover of pleasures,
who sit securely,
who say in your heart,
'I am, and there is no one besides me;
I shall not sit as a widow
or know the loss of children':
These two things shall come to you
in a moment, in one day;
the loss of children and widowhood
shall come upon you in full measure.

ISAIAH 47:8–9

The sons of those who oppressed you
shall come bending low to you;
and all who despised you
shall bow down at your feet;

. . . .

The least one shall become a clan,
and the smallest one a mighty nation;
I am the Lord;
in its time I will hasten it.

ISAIAH 60:14, 22

You shall no more be termed Forsaken,
and your land shall no more be termed Desolate;
but you shall be called My delight is in her,
and your land Married;
for the Lord delights in you,
and your land shall be married.

ISAIAH 62:4

Therefore all who devour you shall be devoured,
and all your foes, every one of them, shall go into
    captivity;
those who despoil you shall become a spoil,
and all who prey on you I will make a prey.

JEREMIAH 30:16

Thus says the Lord: Behold, what I have built I am
breaking down, and what I have planted I am plucking
up.

JEREMIAH 45:4

Babylon must fall for the slain of Israel,
as for Babylon have fallen the slain of all the earth.

JEREMIAH 51:49

And I will have pity on Not pitied,
and I will say to Not my people,
'You are my people' . . .

HOSEA 2:23

Yet I destroyed the Amorite before them,
whose height was like the height of the cedars,
and who was as strong as the oaks;
I destroyed his fruit above,
and his roots beneath.

. . . .

Behold, I will press you down in your place,
as a cart full of sheaves presses down.
Flight shall perish from the swift,
and the strong shall not retain his strength,
nor shall the mighty save his life.

AMOS 2:9, 13–14

Rejoice not over me, O my enemy;
when I fall, I shall rise;
when I sit in darkness,
the Lord will be a light to me.

MICAH 7:8

The pride of your heart has deceived you,
you who live in the clefts of the rock,
whose dwelling is high,
who say in your heart,
'Who will bring me down to the ground?'
Though you soar aloft like the eagle,
though your nest is set among the stars,
thence I will bring you down,
says the Lord.

OBADIAH 3–4

For not from the east or from the west
and not from the wilderness comes lifting up;
but it is God who executes judgment,
putting down one and lifting up another.

PSALM 75:6–7

The stone which the builders rejected
has become the head of the corner.
This is the Lord's doing;
it is marvellous in our eyes.

PSALM 118:22–23

He that goes forth weeping,
bearing the seed for sowing,
shall come home with shouts of joy,
bringing his sheaves with him.

PSALM 126:6

And so one could go on, almost indefinitely. There is one more passage, however, which I must quote; and not only because of the completeness with which it records Yahweh's activities as the God of transposition and revolutionary change; the God who turns everything upside down and inside out. It is the hymn of praise to Yahweh which is put in the mouth of Hannah, the mother of Samuel, after she had waited so long to bear a son; phrases from it were to be incorporated in the "Magnificat" with which another mother, in the Gospel of Luke, expresses her gratitude for the child she is carrying.

> Talk no more so very proudly,
> let not arrogance come from your mouth;
> for the Lord is a God of knowledge,
> and by him actions are weighed.
> The bows of the mighty are broken,
> but the feeble gird on strength.
> Those who were full have hired themselves out for
> bread,
> but those who were hungry have ceased to hunger.
> The barren has borne seven,
> but she who has many children is forlorn.
> The Lord kills and brings to life;
> he brings down to Sheol and raises up.
> The Lord makes poor and makes rich;
> he brings low, he also exalts.
> He raises up the poor from the dust;
> he lifts the needy from the ash heap,
> to make them sit with princes and inherit a seat of
> honour.
> For the pillars of the earth are the Lord's,
> and on them he has set the world.
>
> 1 SAMUEL 2:3–8

One of the most affecting aspects of this hymn is the way in which it "steadies itself" in the last couple of clauses.

Everything, it says, may be in motion, variable, unpredictable; but the world as a whole nevertheless stands firm. (Other Psalms put the same thought in slightly different words. For example: "Yea, the world is established; it shall never be moved"—Psalm 93:1.) Yet it is clear that God is praised here not just as a God of upheaval but *because* he is the God of upheaval; because the writer finds so satisfying ethically and emotionally God's manifesting himself through the ever-altering fortunes of his subjects. In Egyptian texts, we are told by two well-known scholars (H. and H. A. Frankfort in *Before Philosophy*), the "disturbance of the established social order was viewed with horror"; whereas here, they say, it is presented as the proof of the limitlessness of God's power. But the unmistakable note of exultation which sounds through the hymn is a tribute not only to the omnipotence of God, but also to the uses to which he puts it. The disturbance of the social order which the hymn describes is looked upon, quite simply, as evidence of God's indefatigable eagerness to do justice— at all times, and in all places, and to all his subjects.

Now, whatever the real provenance of the hymn may be, in speaking these verses Hannah is supposedly celebrating a personal triumph over adversity. Having been barren for so many years, she has every reason to exult in her God's eagerness to reverse the conditions she had previously known and the expectations everyone presumably had of her. Something of the same sort might be said of many of the prophetic utterances quoted above: for the most part they are prognostications of Israel's recovery from the disasters which had overwhelmed it, and of its eventual triumph over its enemies. It might be asked what prognostications of this kind have to do with any abstract or universally recognizable notion of justice. Why should the understandable desire of the underdog to become top dog in his turn, and his beseeching of his God to secure this great change for him, be dignified with terms that do not really describe it or apply to it? Can any generalized conception of justice or evenhandedness really be seen to be at stake here?

One answer to this question is that even in the most vengeful and ardent of the prophecies of redemption, the action of God in overturning the state of affairs which prevails at any particular moment is never spoken of as "one-off"; it is invariably presented as characteristic of the way in which he has always acted. All the historical books which are the context of the prophecies, and give them much of their authority, show this to be the case. In fact, the ecstatic hopes of revenge and redress which the prophets put forward would have had no imaginative plausibility had they not had behind them the accumulated weight of the entire, centuries-old story of success and defeat, of reward and punishment, of choice and rejection, which the historical narratives had presented.

Even in these utterances, therefore, it can be seen that while the explicit moral goes one way *(Israel will triumph eventually, and forever)*, the hidden moral, or what is called nowadays the "subtext," goes another: *Nothing that this God does or creates is permanent except the world itself, which is the arena of all his actions.*

To give a chapter the title "Peripeteia" is of course to invoke Aristotle's discussion of tragedy in the *Poetics*. There he defines tragedy as a "representation" of a "change in fortune from prosperity to misery, due not to depravity but to some great error" on the part of a highly placed individual; this change from one state of affairs to its opposite being one which "conforms to probability or necessity."

Obviously such a definition of tragedy, as well as the Aristotelian definition of a satisfactory tragic plot ("a unified whole . . . whose various incidents must be so arranged so that if any one of them is differently placed or taken away the effect of wholeness will be seriously disrupted"), refers to something very different from "the story of the stories" in the Hebrew Scriptures. However, the allusion may serve as a reminder that many of the preoccupations of the biblical writers are not as specialized as my account of them, or their own account of them, has perhaps suggested. Peripeteia, a sudden reversal of fortune in the affairs of man, has been a subject for people of all cultures to ponder over and moralize about—inevitably, given the uncertainty of our fates at all times. The prophets' obsession with it is singular in kind, though; and this for two reasons. Firstly, they look at it "collectively." Though the analogies they use to describe it are often taken from private life, and though personifications of abstract, quasi-political forces appear in their poems, they are almost exclusively concerned with the fate of nations, not of individuals. The psychology of peripeteia exists in their work merely in order to make more vivid the politics of peripeteia. (This is not the case with many of the most "personal" of the Psalms.) Secondly, the prophets allow for no element of chance in the understanding of the phenomenon. It always takes place as a result of the action of their God: usually as his punishment for depravity (when you go down), or his reward for virtue and fidelity (when you go up). Sometimes it is simply a consequence of his cunning use of you as instrument (when, as happens with the enemies of Israel, you don't really know what you are about).

Another theme appearing in the prophets' work with which all cultures and religions are preoccupied is that of the inexorable cycle of death and rebirth in nature and human society. (It is in itself a form of peripeteia.) Legends of divine enactments of this cycle, and human mimickings of it, were at the heart of the mysteries and rituals of many of the Near Eastern and Attic religions. Osiris, Tammuz, Adonis, Attis, Dionysus, etc., are all slain; they all rise again; hence the "dying god" so beloved of one school of writers on Middle Eastern mythology. (And so influential, incidentally, on the course of twentieth-century literature. T. S. Eliot, Thomas Mann, and D. H. Lawrence all made self-conscious use of these legends in their work.) Again, the biblical writers gave their treatment of the theme a singular twist. In the Hebrew version of the story of death and regeneration it is not God that dies: he remains inviolate, eternal, transcendent, never himself a part of the processes of nature and history. Rather, he directs them all; and it is the *nation* which in effect goes through the cycle of dismemberment and rebirth; not annually or seasonally, as in the case of the pagan gods, but over great epochs of history.

This Israelite version of the story, modified through the apocalyptic tradition, was eventually to be married to the legends and rituals of the neighboring faiths, and thus to produce the Christian religion. Like the other gods, Jesus is slain, and rises again; unlike them, he goes through his ordeal and subsequent triumph as the redeemer of Israel who had been promised by the prophets and was now transformed into a divine being; indeed, into an aspect of God. His death and resurrection could therefore be presented as the complete and final summation of the nation's history. The fact that for many centuries before Jesus' coming the truly chosen of Israel had been instructed to recognize themselves through the sufferings and humiliations they had to endure, rather than through glory they were able to enjoy, helped to give this twist to the story much of its plausibility. Undergoing the pains of death and dissolution had become the incontestable guarantee of better things to come. Proclamations of the blessings conferred on Yahweh's elect had given way to utterances like "Blessed is the man whom thou dost chasten" (Psalm 94:10)—a sentiment which is to be found also in Proverbs (3:12), in the letter to the Hebrews (12:6), and in the Revelation of John (3:19). Within a single, continuous narrative the Hebrew Scriptures endeavor to describe how and why that very change had come about; and at what cost, and to whose ultimate profit. Then the apocalyptic writers had continued the tale in their own terms, which were even more extravagant than those of the original.

The anomalies and contradictions which a change of this kind inevitably produced—how, for example, can one tell the punishments which God metes out to sinners and blasphemers from the punishments he makes his favored ones endure?—were mediated through concepts like contrition, humility, and faith. These concepts are to be found in a more or less developed form in the prophets and the Psalms; all of them were to undergo a process of elaboration, refinement, and individualization in the years of trial which followed upon the Greek and Roman conquests of the land of Israel. (It is said that the first true religious martyrs to appear in any historical records are those whose deaths are described in the Apocryphal books of the Maccabbees.) The way was thus opened to the Beatitudes of the Sermon on the Mount, where the idea of a national salvation arising out of the sufferings of the nation seems to have yielded wholly to a preoccupation with individual suffering and salvation; and where the state of lowliness and disadvantage is given a virtually "independent" or autonomous moral standing. So far from being seen as a punishment, it is presented as good in itself and of itself; it is regarded as indivisible from the qualities of mercy and righteousness. Yet what it leads to, as in all the prophetic and apocalyptic writings, remains the promise of a great reversal to come.

> Blessed are the poor in spirit, for theirs is the kingdom of heaven.
> Blessed are those who mourn, for they shall be comforted.
> Blessed are the meek, for they shall inherit the earth.
> Blessed are those who hunger and thirst for righteousness, for they shall be satisfied.
> Blessed are the merciful, for they shall obtain mercy.
> Blessed are the pure in heart, for they shall see God.
> Blessed are the peacemakers, for they shall be called sons of God.
> Blessed are those who are persecuted for righteousness' sake, for theirs is the kingdom of heaven.
> Blessed are you when men revile you and persecute you and utter all kinds of evil against you falsely on my account. Rejoice and be glad, for your reward is great in heaven, for so men persecuted the prophets who were before you.
>
> MATTHEW 5:3-11

Again, later in the same Gospel, we find: "But many that are first will be last, and the last first" (19:30), and "Whoever would be great among you must be your servant, and whoever would be first among you must be your slave" (20:26). By this time, with reversals and inversions following so fast upon another, it should not surprise us that a passage which the Jewish psalmist had composed to console his dispirited people—"The stone which the builder rejected has become the head of the corner"—is used by the Gospel writer to prove that the Jews had forfeited forever their chosen status: "*Therefore,*" his interpretation of this verse runs, "I tell you, the kingdom of God will be taken from you and given to a nation producing the fruits of it" (21:43). Since the malefactor who had endured the "shame" of the cross was said to have risen to become the redeemer of all mankind, and not just of Israel, it followed that the Gentiles who had previously been "rejected" were now to become the cornerstones of the arch.

The essential formal principle of Hebrew poetry has long been known as "parallelism of members": that is, "the parallelism of two clauses of approximately the same length, the second clause answering, or otherwise completing, the first" (*Introduction to the Literature of the Old Testament*, by S. R. Driver). Even the most cursory reader of the Hebrew Scriptures, or of the quotations from them in the preceding pages, will know at once what this means. Since the use of this poetic technique was apparently widespread throughout the ancient Near East, any attempt to relate it directly to particular religious and moral patterns or preoccupations within the Hebrew world view is a very chancy business. Yet the attempt has often been made. For example, in *Vom Geist der ebräischen Poesie*, first published in 1783, J. G. Herder says of it (my translation): "The parallelism between heaven and earth goes through all the songs of praise. . . . The purpose of this poetry is to compare the infiniteness of heaven with the mote-like earth; to portray heaven's loftiness against our littleness. . . . The sky alters and changes like a backcloth; the earth is a showplace of phantoms, empty appearances, a graveyard; but the God of heaven and earth, who was present before the mountains existed, remains with eternity. . . . Through parallelism we are led to compare the infinite and the finite; to bring together the immeasurably vast and nothing."

And much more to the same effect. One may set against this the view of the Frankforts, in the book cited earlier in this chapter, who speak of parallelism in Egyptian verse as symptomatic of the Egyptian sense of "balance, symmetry, and geometry"; they believe the regard which the Egyptians had for these qualities to be visible not only in the verse form, but also in their art and architecture, as well as in their theology and ethics. Or one may set against both these views that of D. H. Lawrence: in a deleted section from *Apocalypse*, which has been printed in the new, complete edition of his works, he refers to the "image-rhythm" of parallelism as a "perpetual yet unexpected antiphony, like the strong heart-beat followed by the weak." (And from what depth in Lawrence's imagination *that* image emerged we can judge from the following passage in *Sons and Lovers*, written more than a quarter of a century before, which describes Paul Morel with his dying mother: "He stood looking out of the window. The whole country was bleak and pallid under the snow. Then he felt her pulse. There was a strong stroke and a weak one, like a sound and its echo. That was supposed to betoken the end. She let him feel her wrist, knowing what he wanted.")

To this very small sampling of some possible responses to the prosodic device or technique of parallelism, I would like to add my own, briefly. It is simply that parallelism, of its very nature, was peculiarly suitable for the expression of that sense of a "mutual" peripeteia—of reciprocity, in other words—which I have been trying to define in these pages, and which seems to me central to the story told in the Scriptures. Through their echoic effects the couplets and triplets generate a feeling of change within likeness, and of likeness within change, that is itself like the never-ending rise and fall of the fortunes and the emotions which they depict. Everything in these verses rises in order to fall, and falls in order to rise again: inexorably, turn and turn about, for as long as history endures. As with the earth itself in Hannah's hymn of praise, there is no rest or permanence within this poetic form: for that very reason, strangely enough, it becomes what the prophet Jeremiah called "a habitation of justice."

CHAPTER ELEVEN

ETHICS, FANTASY, AND HISTORY

There are laws—and laws. There are God's explicit edicts, which govern the forms of the worship he expects, as well as the relations between the people of Israel and others, and among the Israelites themselves. It is the operation in history of these laws that the story is intended to make clear: as often as not, by revealing the consequences of their infraction. But there are laws of another kind which the story contains and is contained by. Implicit laws, these are; unconscious laws (if that is a permissible phrase) or laws of the unconscious; laws which reveal the very limits of our language and the mind's capacity to formulate moral and intellectual concepts—which is exactly where one should expect to find a god at work! Of these laws, the one which is central to this discussion is the law of reciprocity—for which another name might be the law of choice and rejection. The God of Israel rejects *because*s he chooses. He has to. How can he not? Who can imagine choice without rejection? The same is true of all the other necessary consequences of his moral habits. He humbles because he exalts; he retracts because he gives; he even hates because he loves. Inevitably, his own people, the ones he had chosen above all others, were bound to have the most comprehensive opportunity of learning all this about him and from him; they had to have the lessons they learned scored on their flesh. "You only have I known of all the families of earth; therefore do I visit upon you all your iniquities" (Amos 3:2).

A problem that remains, however, is the relationship between the two kinds of laws postulated above: between those which are supposedly formulated and delivered to his people by Yahweh, and those which are inherent and yet unacknowledged in the very conception of such a God; the laws which define his nature, one might say, rather than the ones which he defines for his people. What is the relationship between them? On the one hand, the successive reversals of attitude to his people and to others through which God reveals his nature, and which produce the endless to and fro of history, appear to be impersonal, mechanical, ineluctable, pendulum-like. They happen because they have to happen, God being what he is; they will happen eternally, or at any rate until he brings history to a halt. (And one cannot help wondering: what task will be left for him to perform then?) On the other hand, there are all the detailed edicts that God issues to his people— some of which are cultic, but many of which are ethical in character. How do these different spheres of activity or of being intersect with one another? How does the domain of historical necessity relate to the domain of the ethical, especially; to the ideas of justice and compassion which figure so largely in the Scriptures?

Well, I have already given some examples of the way in which that relationship may be said to work; and "work" is a key word here, since it implies not a replication of elements, or a simple cause-and-effect relationship of the kind the biblical writers themselves put forward, but an active transformation, or reordering, or inversion, of material in its passage from one domain to another. I suggested, for instance, that the arbitrariness of God's initial choice of Israel, and his gift to the people of Israel of a land that belonged to others, were elements in the tale that the biblical myth attempted not so much to conceal as to control. Through the covenant, and through the institution of the Law, the attempt was made to rationalize, to moralize, even to "juridicalize," the will of God; to render it answerable to the demands for predictability and reliability without which the Israelites could hardly have recognized themselves as a historic community.

But those selfsame demands reveal that alongside the gratitude that was felt toward God for the favors he had done for the people, there ran other emotions: fears, compunctions, guilts, self-doubts, and the like. How could the dangers of what he had done not be present in the minds of Yahweh's subjects? Aggression, to put it simply, produced an inevitable, reciprocal fear of retribution. From "him"? Or from all those other people whom he had not chosen? From those who had been rejected and were therefore to be despised? From those who were being driven out of their land at his behest? How can one distinguish between "him" and "them," the others, the enemies, the rejected ones? To ask for favors is to become conscious of those at whose expense they are to be granted; to receive them exposes you to the danger of losing them. All this, too, had to be controlled and rationalized; it, too, had to be incorporated into the overall myth. Hence the readiness—the "inevitability," as we say—with which God turns away from his chosen people, and inflicts upon them the sufferings that have to be gone through by those whom he has rejected.

To put it simply again: if your good means the harm of others, you know that they will feel about it exactly as you would if they had been chosen and you had been rejected. Even in your moment of triumph you know it; or just after, anyway. And you know it because there is an irrefragable identity or community of human feeling between you and them, whoever they may be. The double nature of this identity of feeling, and the double nature of its consequences, must not be misunderstood, however. The consciousness that you may share the disagreeable fate of your victim, and the knowledge from within yourself, as it were, of what he is feeling, are as likely to produce a fixed determination on your part to keep him where he is, as it is to generate the wish to moderate or alleviate his sufferings. You can always try to deny the humanity which, at another level, you know you share with him. In the Hebrew Scriptures we can see all those impulses expressed: the compassionate or protective ("You know the heart of the stranger, for you were strangers in the land of Egypt"); and the guiltily vindictive. In much the same way, *being* the victim or loser will produce a hunger for justice that is virtually indistinguishable from a dream of revenge and recompense; these, too, are to be found in the Scriptures.

Usually we are inclined to think of fantasy simply as an expression of a desire to escape from the constraints of morality, as well as from all the other social and physical constraints which bind us. That is certainly one of its functions. But considered from another point of view, fantasy is itself the creator of some of the constraints from which it seems to offer us a temporary escape. This is especially true of our sense of the reality of other people's lives to *them:* which is the foundation of every kind or degree of moral awareness. Through fantasy we "put ourselves in their place," as we say, or we put them provisionally in our place: an involuntary activity of the mind to which we owe the capacity to feel compassion, as well as the capacity to take pleasure in the sufferings and deprivations of others. We cannot, in the nature of the case, and in the nature of the race, feel the one without being able to feel the other. That is how ambiguous we are as moral beings. (I am speaking of the race, I repeat, not of individuals, in whom these capacities will always be unevenly mixed; so that at either extreme there are people who appear to be without any admixture of what is to be found at the other extreme.) Sadism, in these terms, is as "imaginative" as compassion; it, too, depends on the re-creation within one consciousness of what is going on in the nervous system of another.

The borderline between fantasy and the moral life, then, is everywhere and nowhere. Neither could exist without the other. They support each other even—or perhaps especially—when they are at war with one another. The process of mutual recoil and interpenetration between them is a never-ending one. All stories—myths, legends, fairy tales, epics, novels, plays—are a record of it. They are fantasies, yes. But they differ from most idle daydreams and wish fulfillments in incorporating the moral anxieties which they themselves have aroused. They carry as much as they can bear of the complexities and obduracies of the experience from which they initially appeared to offer a retreat: this by way of rebuke for the wishes revealed within them; as well as of promise that further comforting flights or indulgences of fancy are now permissible. In any elaborate story there are obscure centers of feeling in which rebuke is in fact a mode of wish fulfillment, and wish fulfillment a form of rebuke.

To return to Yahweh and the people of Israel, and to the different sets of "laws" which appear to govern the domains of historical reciprocity and reversibility, on the one hand, and the domain of ethics, on the other hand, I am saying, in effect, that so far from being mechanical or impersonal, the laws of the first kind embody a *moral* interpretation of the world and of the events that take place within it. They are moral, that is, in the sense defined above: they are a precipitate of profound conflicts of desire and anxiety on the part of the writers. They are born out of a conviction—often a reluctant or angered conviction—of an ineluctable similarity of sentiment between all men; of their common vulnerability to misfortune, and of the likelihood that they will feel their misfortunes in an identical way. The iron laws of reciprocity and reversibility have their origin not in the nature of things, but in the moral and emotional misgivings of the man who wishes his group to prosper above all others. If "nature" is in question, it is human nature that these laws reveal, not the nature of the universe, or of a fixed, given, self-defining set of historical events.

It should hardly be necessary to say it, but let it be said, nevertheless: There was no compulsion from without upon the writers to see their history in the terms in which it is presented in the Hebrew Scriptures. They themselves created the patterns of reciprocity (and the accompanying "narrative compulsions") that have been looked at in earlier chapters; these patterns lay within the logic of their own tale and the lessons it was intended to enforce, not out there, inertly, in the logic of history itself. There is nothing special in the fact that the people of Israel knew both success and failure in the course of their history. About what people could that not be said? What was special—unique, indeed—about the spokesmen of this people was the way in which they accounted, through the actions of their God, for success and failure; the interpretations and explanations they offered of his actions, the moral teachings they drew from them, and the expectations they nourished as a result.

To create a single and solitary God who reveals himself by means of a series of irreversible acts in the history of one particular people whom he has chosen for himself, and who intends a particular "end" to the historical processes which he has initiated, is necessarily to create a God of instability, of interrelated better and worse fortunes, of rewards and punishments; it is to see his world, as long as history continues, as a place in which no perfect equilibrium is attainable, since everything in it, your own people included, has constantly to rise and fall in relation to everything else. How else, the welfare of nations being peculiarly his care, could he show pleasure or displeasure? Thus it is that among the variety of moral codes which the actions of such a God would seem to underwrite—and I emphasize it is only one possibility among others—is the code which eventually found explicit expression with Jesus, and with his contemporary Rabbi Hillel: the ethics of the Golden Rule, the ethics of "Do as you would be done by."

Do as you would be done by? Time, or history, according to the laws of reciprocity, is going to make sure that that is exactly what happens anyway. As you did, so will it be done to you. As others did to you, so will it be done to

them. This process will go on while time and history endure;
for they, and God himself, come close to being all one.

> For the day of the Lord is near upon all the nations.
> As you have done, it shall be done to you,
>   your deeds shall return on your own head.
>   OBADIAH 1:15

CHAPTER TWELVE

THE ONENESS
OF YAHWEH

As a projection of human needs and fears Yahweh had a great advantage over all his divine predecessors and contemporaries. He was one: a single, solitary being. All the emotions of his people had to be focused upon him; he alone was responsible for the moral and cultic codes by which they were instructed to live; there could be no appeal beyond him. The fact that he was temperamentally so variable—kind and ruthless, protective and angry, remorseless and yet swayed by contrition or appeals to his pride, triumphant and humble—could not lead to a process of fission or splintering from within, precisely because there was no recourse beyond him; he was always ultimately in charge, answerable only to himself. Imaginatively speaking, his emotional mutability actually increased the power available to him. His laws remained unfathomable and unarguable, since they proceeded directly from him; yet he was also "human," all too fatherlike, a changeable being with whom it was possible to have discourse, however one-sided its terms.

The phrase "a single God" or "one God" carries within it a reference to at least two overlapping areas of meaning, which have to be distinguished from one another. It can

refer either to his solitude as the object of his people's worship, or to what might be called his "substance"—the unity
of his spiritual composition; of that which he is. As far as
the question of God's substance is concerned, it is not surprising that we can find little or no speculation on the
subject in the Hebrew Scriptures; it was not the kind of
topic for which they even appear to have had a vocabulary.
What there are instead are hints—especially in the tales
of the patriarchs, but in later episodes as well—of the existence of certain other, more material or phenomenal gods
who had been absorbed into Yahweh: a storm god or volcano
god who appears in the Sinai; a travelers' or nomads' war
god who moves about with the Ark; perhaps a bull god
in the days of Jeroboam, in which form some scholars believed him to have been worshiped in the northern kingdom; and so forth.

Highly refined displays of learning and speculation on
these matters can be found in many scholarly works. However, just as successive generations of biblical writers and
editors knitted together an immense variety of material from
different sources into one ever-expanding narrative, so the
earlier fragmented versions of other gods discernible in the
text contributed to a conception of the God as a single,
spiritual being, which was itself undergoing a constant process of elaboration and expansion. If Yahweh was to answer
the pressing needs of his people at different stages of their
history, he was bound to manifest himself to them in many
different modes or moods; at the same time, the momentum
of the narrative was sustained by and limited by the unfolding of potentialities which only a solitary God could have
possessed. Thus he could absorb other gods; he could never
share power with them or distribute himself or his qualities
among them. And at all times, whether he appears as the

tribal God of battles, or as the righteous and universalist God of the prophets, he had to be active, interventionist, creative, and initiatory; a God who reveals his innermost nature through his actions. He was what he did. His being and his doing were one. *That* was the mode of his unity within himself: a unity not so much of divine "substance" or "spirit" as of deed. Even the words directly ascribed to him by Moses, or the chroniclers, or the prophets, are invariably either instructions to his auditors or accounts of his past, present, and future actions.

Which brings us to the other area of reference implicit in the phrase "one God"—the solitariness, or otherwise, of the deity as the object of just one people's worship, initially; and then as the creator of the world and the ruler of all mankind. In terms of the entire story, the movement from the first role to the second is also an example of the necessary, inevitable unfolding of a potentiality. If Yahweh permitted his people to worship no god but himself—and we know that there was nothing about which he was more "jealous"—then what was he to do when he and they encountered other gods of other peoples? (Which they did from the very beginning.) He had to assert his superiority over them. What would be the good of him if he did not? Implicit in that assertion, however, lay his denying the reality of all other gods even for other peoples: which is a rather different and even more far-reaching claim. Sooner or later, events were bound to elicit it from him. The spiritual-political "imperialism" which the biblical writers engaged in on their God's behalf left him, as it were, with no alternative.

Having put the word "imperialism" in quotation marks in the last sentence, I now withdraw not the word but the marks. In the ancient Near East, gods were habitually envisaged as kings; and kings as gods or demigods. Gods had to be praised in the language of kingship, and kings in the language of the divine. All else aside, it seems that men have only a limited stock of words and images with which to express flattery, fear, self-abasement, vicarious pride, wonder, and a sense of participatory glory in displays of power. Unlike their neighbors, the Israelites never confused their kings with their undivided and fiercely jealous God; he would not have tolerated such a confusion. (Though it can be seen creeping in, with momentous consequences, in those late apocalyptic texts which impute a supernatural status of some kind to the long-awaited Messiah.) But they did think of their God as though he were a king, both on earth and in heaven, and praised him as such; and they did as a matter of course run together the idea of Israel's dominion over its neighbors with that of Yahweh's dominion over foreign peoples.

In that respect their language was like their neighbors'. But whereas the kings, priests, and praise-singers of the Egyptians and the various Mesopotamian empires obviously had a great deal to boast about, in speaking of the regions to which they had carried their gods, the imperialism of the Israelite God was, at its most intense moments, born of humiliation and defeat: it was merely a dream imperialism; the imperialism of impotent fantasy.

Merely! There are many things to be learned from the Hebrew and Christian Scriptures. Perhaps the most important of them all is never to despise the power of dreams. Especially of those dreams which deny the veracity of everyone else's.

The singularity of Yahweh (in every sense of the phrase) is wholly dependent upon his transcendence; his transcendence is dependent upon his solitariness. Were he in any way a part of, and hence subject to, the processes of nature; were he to feed, or breed, or die, or be born again in some form different from the one he had had before, or even in the same form as before, he would need the help of other gods and of men to perform his tasks and go through these transformations. Equally, because he has no peers, no rivals, no fellows to keep him company or with whom to quarrel or cooperate, he is bound to remain above and outside all that he created. Even when he manifests himself within that creation, he never actually becomes the phenomenon through which he makes himself known, whatever it may be—storm, volcano, burning bush, human dream.

Sometimes it is possible to see God struggling to achieve and retain his transcendence; just as he can sometimes be seen coalescing different forms or aspects of himself in order to become and remain one; or be seen engaged in widening the area over which he rules in solitude. But the glimpses we are afforded of an immanent (indwelling) God are of no more consequence, ultimately, than those we have of a divided God. Other gods are themselves aspects of the world: they bow over it, as sky; or they lie prostrate at the base of it, as earth; or sway to and fro in space, as water; or ride over it, as the sun; or are born willy-nilly as a result of cosmic acts of fornication. But not this one. The world remains throughout nothing more than a manifestation of his power. He is, therefore, set free from it. Everything he says and every hymn of praise addressed to him contains the implication that he could have abstained from the original act of creation, had he so wished; or that he could destroy his own creation, if the desire moved him.

He *chose* to make the world! Only a transcendent God could have had so free a choice in the matter. In Chapter Three ("The Choice"), I described Yahweh as an "inveterate or compulsive chooser," whose freedom of action was constrained in one respect only: he was *not* free not to choose. Many instances were given of his manner of choosing among nations, individuals, places, foods, and so forth; connected with these, I suggested, was the fact that Yahweh did not live in the land he had chosen for his people, but had to arrive in it with them. Anterior to all the choices of the kind mentioned above, it must now be said of him, lay a greater choice still, the greatest of all possible choices: whether or not to bring the world into being; and having done so, whether or not to sustain it in existence. That choice, too, is presented as an arbitrary exercise of will on his part, like his election of the people of Israel. We are given no reason why he creates heaven and earth, but are told only of each act of creation and of the achievement overall that he "saw that it was good." We are also told that he is frequently tempted to reconsider this view, in the light of man's behavior.

In saying that God's choosing to create the world was "anterior" to the other acts of choosing through which he revealed his nature, I am not necessarily speaking of how the record of his actions was compiled. The idea of a God who is at all times above or beyond the world which he had chosen to create did not have to precede the birth of a God who was free to choose Israel to be his own possession among the nations. That is not how the minds of the biblical writers worked. But the connection between these two ideas is plain. If Yahweh's singularity and his transcendence depend upon one another, then these attributes also exist in a state of mutual dependence with his power of exercising choice in the most momentous matters, as in the most trivial.

The same might be said of another aspect of God, which perhaps appears remote from these considerations: his "formlessness." In this respect Yahweh once more shows himself to be wholly unlike any other god of the time and place in which he appeared, or of virtually all times and places since. It is true that insofar as the biblical writers visualized their God, they obviously conceived him as having the appearance, as well as the emotions and (in some sense) the thoughts, of a man: this is the case not just with certain primitively anthropomorphic notions to be found in the early legends incorporated in Genesis, say, or of the entire system of sacrifice and burnt offering which was central to the cult of Yahweh in the Temple and elsewhere, but also of prophets like Isaiah, Jeremiah, and Ezekiel. All of these heard his voice; they all speak of his hands; at least two of them saw him seated on a throne in "a likeness as it were of a human form" (Ezekiel 1:26). And the Psalms abound in directly anthropomorphic images of all kinds. Indeed, it is a commonplace among religious writers to claim that the "individuality" of Yahweh, the strength of the "personhood" he possessed, were of great significance in the development of the ethical and emotional relationship which men were able to have with him.

If, then, he is so much like a person, how can he also be described as formless? The answer is: because of his prohibition of the making of graven images of any kind, including of course images of himself. What it suggests is that people must not seek to make final or definite their visions of him, or declare them to be authentic renderings of what cannot in fact be rendered physically. (It is striking that in the verbal representations of Yahweh much is always left vague, as we can see from the last citation from Ezekiel. In the verses describing Yahweh and the heavenly hosts in Chapter 6 of Isaiah, the prophet tells us only that the Lord was "high and lifted up"; the description of the seraphim is much more detailed.) The prohibition against the making of images is not intended merely to guard against the possibility of the devotions that are due Yahweh being transferred to some secondhand and hence fraudulent representation of him; nor is it intended just to mark off his difference from all the inferior gods of other peoples, who could be so represented. Both these considerations are important; yet they must be seen not only in relation to Yahweh's solitude, and the jealousy which goes with it, but also in relation to his transcendence, and the power which goes with that. To represent is to limit. Only that which is finite is capable of being represented in plastic form; whatever is subject to bounds cannot be all-powerful.

Yahweh's chief "characteristic" or attribute is his power, from beginning to end. He nevers loses it. He loses his temper; he changes his mind (even though from time to time he is made to ask scornfully of his interlocutors if they imagine him to be a man who can be diverted from his purposes); he loses the loyalty of his people; for their part, they lose almost everything he had promised them (on conditions). But the power imputed to him never lessens or slackens. On the contrary, it grows and grows; and it never grows so rapidly as when his people is defeated and sent into exile, and the Temple built for his worship is reduced to ashes.

One thing the biblical writers cannot be accused of is levity. Jokes are not their forte. The nearest they come to what might be called humor is their penchant for irony. In the histories and biographies, as well as in the overall "story of the stories," dramatic ironies abound; in the prophetic writings a persistent use is made of rhetorical ironies of all kinds—sarcasm, invective, mock-incomprehension, the habit of "leading on" the reader to nourish expectations which are then savagely revealed to be illusory.

Hardly any subject more readily brings out the ironist in the prophets than the worship of idols or graven images. In each case the scorn expressed is focused on the idea of a man worshiping something which he knows to have been made by himself or by other men. No doubt because it would complicate issues too much, the writers do not acknowledge the possibility that the idol might be worshiped precisely as a representation or temporary habitation of the god, and not as the god itself.

> He cuts down cedars; or he chooses a holm tree or an oak and lets it grow strong among the trees of the forest; he plants a cedar and the rain nourishes it. Then it becomes fuel for a man; he takes a part of it and warms himself, he kindles a fire and bakes bread; also he makes a god and worships it, he makes it a graven image and falls down before it. Half of it he burns in the fire; over the half he eats flesh, he roasts meat and is satisfied; also he warms himself and says, 'Aha, I am warm, I have seen the fire!' And the rest of it he makes into a god, his idol; and falls down to it and worships it; he prays to it and says, 'Deliver me, for thou art my god!'
>
> ISAIAH 44:14–17

> A tree from the forest is cut down,
> and worked with an axe by the hands of a craftsman.
> Men deck it with silver and gold;
> they fasten it with hammer and nails

so that it cannot move.
Their idols are like scarecrows in a cucumber field,
and they cannot speak;
they have to be carried,
for they cannot walk.
Be not afraid of them,
for they cannot do evil,
neither is it in them to do good.

JEREMIAH 10:3–5

What profit is an idol
when its maker has shaped it,
a metal image, a teacher of lies?
For the workman trusts in his own creation
when he makes dumb idols!
Woe to him who says to a wooden thing, Awake;
to a dumb stone, Arise!
Can this give revelation?
Behold, it is overlaid with gold and silver,
and there is no breath at all in it.

HABBAKUK 2:18–19

Long before Xenophanes' declaration that if horses had hands and could draw, they would draw their gods in the shape of horses, and long, long before Feuerbach described the deity as an "objectification" of man's "latent nature," some at least of the Israelites were aware of the "god-making" faculties of mankind. Hence their heavy sarcasm about these idols, in comparison with their own invisible and transcendent God. Each of the passages cited above is followed immediately by an invocation of Yahweh's glory and solitude (Isaiah); his "great[ness] in might" (Jeremiah); and his "holy temple" (Habbakuk). However, from our point of view there is a larger and more inclusive irony in such utterances than the one directed by the prophets against their enemies. "Like them be those who make them!" wrote the psalmist of idols and their makers (Psalm 135:17). Yet what, after all, has been the ruling presumption of this book, if not that the writers of the Scriptures, too, were god-makers? They did not use gold, silver, wood, hammered brass, nails, and the rest. The material of which they made their God was words—words expressing emotions we can still be moved by, and ideas of great scope; but drawn from within themselves nevertheless; as human as the smeltings and moldings that produced the gods of Canaan.

Though it has often been said before, it is worth repeating here, finally, that the vitality and individuality of Yahweh as a "person," and hence as a personal deity, seems to have been a precondition for the development among the biblical writers of an interest in *human* motivation and actions that is quite without precedent. "The Patriarchs," writes W. F. Albright in *The Biblical Period from Abraham to Ezra*, "come alive with a vividness unknown to a single extrabiblical character in the whole vast literature of the ancient Near East." The judges, kings, prophets, courtiers, and countrymen who appear in such profusion in the stories to be found in the later historical books show the same qualities. Only Homer (roughly contemporaneous with the documents dating from the eighth and seventh centuries B.C.) can be brought into comparison with them. The subtleties of the narrative techniques employed in the stories are an index of the writers' sophisticated and passionate interest in the psychology of their characters; an interest which their moral and homiletic intentions greatly sharpen.

No justice has been done in the preceding pages to this aspect of the Scriptures. I mention it here to make the point, if only in the most general terms, that "the story of the stories" owes quite as much to the individual tales within it as they owe to it. Everything that has been said about the imaginative autonomy of the myth, its capacity to generate growth from within, applies equally to the units of narrative that help to make it up. They sustain the myth in many ways; not least by striving constantly, if never wholly successfully, to escape from it. The myth enlarged and changed itself to take into account those events in the nation's history which apparently controverted the idea of Yahweh as the special protector of the Israelites and their bringer of victories. In a comparable way, the biographical narratives show Yahweh's omnipotence being repeatedly challenged and tested, if never finally overthrown, by individual Israelites, who became through their own acts and passions whatever they had to be.

CHAPTER THIRTEEN

SOME CHRISTIAN TRANSPOSITIONS

Did Yahweh outgrow his people? History would seem to show that he did. Once he or some aspect of his divinity had been embodied in Jesus, and had undergone the crucifixion and the resurrection—or to put it another way, once the omnipotent, solitary God of Israel, and his servant, the Messiah or national redeemer, had been fused with ideas from Greek philosophy, and with Near Eastern religious practices—he conquered much of the world. As the crucified and resurrected Christ, however, it might be said that he had become so different from Yahweh as to be another deity entirely.

Almost from the very first days there have in fact been Christians who wished their God and their faith to bear as little relation as possible to the Hebrew Scriptures, and to the God and the people who appear in them. Ironically, it is these same Christians, the ones who are most hostile to the inheritance from Israel and wish to repudiate the Israelite God most decisively, who positively *need* the "Old" Testament, and everything they find hateful in it, in order to define what they value most in Christianity. Thus the Christian God of Love is contrasted with the Hebrew God of Law; the Christian "circumcision of the heart" with the Israelite circumcision of the flesh; the sacrifices in the Temple with the unique self-sacrifice of Jesus; the worldly political supremacy sought by the Israelites with the spiritual "Kingdom of God" which is within each one of us . . . and so on, one might say, indefinitely.

Either way, the Jews were bound to be the losers: once, that is, Christianity had survived the persecutions it suffered initially, and had become a successfully proselytizing creed. The Christians who emphasized the connection with the Hebrew Scriptures did so in order to justify and glorify the new religion; they wanted to show that all the promises of the Scriptures had been miraculously fulfilled; fulfilled beyond all possible imaginings. The Jews who were incapable of seeing this great fact had become, therefore, nothing more than the withered branch of a living tree. On the other hand, the Christians who wished to put the greatest possible distance between Yahweh and the newly revealed God would obviously do it in the manner described above: by way of hostile and negative contrast. In addition, there were bound to be those who would move on particular issues from the one attitude to the other, or adopt a variety of intermediate positions, without fully being aware of doing so.

This whole range of attitudes is presented at least *in potentio* in the Gospels and the Acts (and in a rather different way in the Letters). It is impossible to read them without being aware that a war to the death against the parent religion, or what was intended to be a war to the death against it, is being fought within them. (The views of the "historical" Jesus about the religion into which he had been born, and about his coreligionists, are not at issue here. The Gospel writers were facing an entirely different situation from any he had known—not the least difference being the effect of his life and death on *them*.) This "war" is not confined to the passages in the Gospels which show Jesus locked in direct combat with the Jewish religious authorities of the day; or which seek to put the entire guilt of his death on these authorities, together with their supporters in the Jewish "multitude," and so on to their children and children's children; or which show much eagerness to exonerate the Romans from blame. Nor is the "war" confined to the ingenious reasonings and admonishments through which Paul tried to show that the Mosaic Law, and with it the unique status of the Jews in the eyes of their God, had been decisively abrogated or superseded, to the incalculable benefit of all mankind. Nor, again, is it confined to the numberless attempts, especially in Matthew, to "match" the details of Jesus' life and death to specific promises and references in the Psalms and prophecies, with the intention of proving that these had now exhausted themselves, as it were, or had been exhausted by events: the future of which they had spoken being the one that was already accomplished.

The propagandistic effect of all this is immense; and has often been remarked on. (Though not as often as it has been taken at face value!) The same intention can of course be seen in some of the parables: like the one about the owner of the vineyard whose tenants beat and stone his servants, and kill his son. " 'When therefore,' " Jesus asks the disciples, " 'the owner of the vineyard comes, what will he do to the tenants?' They said to him, 'He will put those wretches to a miserable death and let out the vineyard to other tenants who will give him the fruits in the season' " (Matthew 21:40–41). Just in case the point is missed, both the narrator and Jesus himself gloss it very firmly: on one side you have the "[foreign] nation" who had previously been "rejected" (the new tenants), and on the other "the chief priests and the Pharisees" (the old tenants, who must be put to death). The parables of the Prodigal Son and of the Good Samaritan are also cases in point. In the latter it is significant that the passerby who succors the injured man is a Samaritan—i.e., *not* a Jew, let alone one of the priests or Levites. ("For Jews have no dealings with the Samaritans," says the fourth chapter of John, describing a meeting between Jesus and yet another strikingly well-disposed Samaritan.) That parable may also be compared with the account of the instant conversion and baptism by Philip of the Ethiopian eunuch whom he encounters on the road to Gaza, in Acts 8.*

The impulse to incorporate into the new religion every-

---

* The parallel between the Good Samaritan and the Ethiopian, in respect of their "foreignness" or "non-Jewishness," may seem farfetched to some. It would not have seemed so to Simone Weil. In *Waiting on God* she invokes the Ethiopian, whom she treats with solemn literalness as a wholly historical figure, as irrefutable "proof" that the Jewish contemporaries of Jesus were far more hardhearted than all other peoples. (Not even the disciples are excluded from this charge.) The elevation of Simone Weil to the status of a kind of twentieth-century Christian saint has not, incidentally, been hindered by her pathological anti-Semitism. On the contrary. The fact that she was Jewish by birth lends it a degree of acceptability or respectability for which some readers are probably grateful.

There are many strata in the Gospels; as one might expect, these strata are severely faulted and buckled, and different elements in them surface at different places; each of the Gospels does not agree with the others over some important issues. Thus it is not surprising that there are certain passages, a few of them quoted from the mouth of Jesus himself, which so far from being anti-Jewish are in fact strongly anti-Gentile. At one point (Mark 7:27) Jesus compares the Gentiles with "dogs"; a couple of times the Samaritans are presented in a bad light; Jesus is said to command his apostles to avoid them and to "go rather to the lost sheep of the house of Israel" (Matthew 10:5–6). These sayings sit so uncomfortably with the theological intentions so clearly present everywhere else in the Gospels—with the writers' anxiety to appeal directly to the Gentiles— that commentators of all denominations are inclined to seize upon them as "bedrock": incontestably genuine utterances, from the original source. They may be so; they may not be. What matters here is that within the context of the narratives overall, this solicitude on Jesus' part toward his own people effectively becomes part of the Gospels' heavy indictment against them. How worthy did they show themselves of his solicitude? How did they repay him for it?

thing of the Jewish/Israelite past which could be usefully incorporated into it, and utterly to annihilate the rest, is dramatized even in some of the miracles said to have been performed by Jesus: most notably perhaps in his cursing of the fig tree that bore no fruit, and that promptly dies as a result of the curse. In both Matthew and Mark, this "fruitless" tree appears in close conjunction with the parable of the vineyard owner and his tenants which is cited above, and thus with the promise that the vineyard will go to other tenants, who will not begrudge the owner its fruits in their season. In Matthew 3:10 we are also told that every tree that does not bear good fruit "is cut down and thrown into the fire." And when Jesus miraculously cures the servant of the Roman centurion as a reward for his faith, Matthew (8:12) has him, by way of contrast, once again consign "the sons of the kingdom" (Israel) to hell: to "the outer darkness" where "men will weep and gnash their teeth." No wonder, given this overall *Tendenz* in the Gospels, that the betrayer of Jesus goes by the generic name of Judas: i.e., Judah; or quite simply, the Jew.*

Animus of this kind did not spring only from what might be called theological considerations; enlightened scholars agree that it also reflected important shifts in the relations between Jews and Romans generally. After the Jewish revolt against Rome had finally been put down in A.D. 73, it became vital for the Christians outside Palestine to distinguish themselves as clearly as possible from the Jews. Otherwise they would have got the worst of both worlds: treated as renegades by the Jews, they were in danger of being treated as Jews, or something worse, by the Romans. Hence the generosity, not to say tenderness, with which the Gospel

---

* To be fair, Luke lists another, wholly inconspicuous Judas (or Thaddaeus, as he is called in Mark and Matthew) among the apostles.

narratives treat particular Romans (from more than one anonymous centurion to the reluctant, kindhearted Procurator), as against their readiness to slander the Jews of Jesus' time and all their succeeding generations. "His blood on us and on our children!" The implausibility of that line did not prevent it from becoming the most disastrously effective utterance in the entire history of propaganda.

Still—to use terms like "propaganda," "animus," and "a war to the death" in describing this aspect of the Christian Scriptures is ultimately misleading, unless the terms are infused with a sense of the inward as well as the external dimensions of the struggle they record. Much of the writers' energy is clearly directed not so much against Jews who denied the messiahship of Jesus as against some of those who had in fact accepted him as the Messiah. There were in Palestine Jewish Christians (the "conservatives," as they might be called), some of whom had been close to Jesus; they wished strenuously to preserve the Jewish Law, and to admit to their ranks only the newcomers who accepted it in its entirety. Against them were ranged the "radicals" (mostly from the Hellenistic Judeo-Christian communities), who wanted to carry the evangel as speedily as possible to all nations, and who regarded the Law as something worse than a shackle or clog on their attempts to accomplish that task. Only the arguments used by the successful faction against the losers are preserved; but they are sufficient to enable one to make out the lines along which the battle was fought.

Yet even that battle is an external affair, compared with another series of desperate engagements that had to be settled before the Christian Scriptures could assume the form they did. I mean by this the struggles that took place within particular individuals between the beliefs they had inherited and the revelation they thought they had been vouchsafed. These could be settled only through the death of *part of themselves;* and the sense of the fatality of the conflict each of them had to go through affects every level of discourse in the Gospels, and the Letters, and the histories and anecdotes in Acts. In the stories they tell, in the doctrines they expound, in the words and imagery they use, they speak of a violent death deliberately sought out and willingly endured, out of which new life and new power are expected to emerge. In such terms some of the earliest Christians present not only the fate of Jesus; but also in effect the historical fate, as they saw it, of the religion of which they had been adherents; and not only the fate of the religion, but also their own fate as individuals. They had to die as Jews—or at the least, some of their deepest expectations as Jews had to die—so that they might be reborn as Christians. "For if we have been united with him in a death like his, we shall certainly be united with him in a resurrection like his" (Romans 6:5). Later they were to die as Christians in order to be reborn as martyrs and saints.

Nothing could illustrate this process more dramatically than Paul's conversion. On the road to Damascus, according to his own account of the event, he mimed his own death as closely as anyone could, without actually dying. For three days after his vision of Jesus ("Saul, Saul, why do you persecute me?") he lay in a coma: blind, speechless, taking no food and drink. "Then he rose and was baptized, and took food and was strengthened. . . . And in the synagogues immediately he proclaimed Jesus, saying, 'He is the Son of God' " (Acts 9:18–20).

That such a man, one who had previously been "a Hebrew

of the Hebrews" and a zealous chastiser of the Christians, became after this experience the most radical among the members of the new sect, and that he should have made the complete abrogation of the Jewish Law, which he had hitherto claimed to uphold so scrupulously, a central feature of his preachings—all that may seem predictable enough, in its way. What is without parallel is the intellectual and emotional intensity with which, as a result of his cataclysmic conversion, he proceeded to put together many if not all of the elaborate, mutually sustaining doctrines of Christianity: original sin, justification through faith, vicarious atonement, the preexistence of Christ, and the like. Into doctrines seemingly as abstract as these all the contradictions and passionate self-divisions of his nature and experience were dissolved or resolved.

What is more—and this is something that relatively few Christian laymen seem to be aware of, however familiar it may be to professionals—this was done without his showing any active interest, apparently, in the teachings and sayings attributed to Jesus, or in any of the events in Jesus' life which preceded the crucifixion. (The final assembly in different forms of the stories in the Gospels, it is fair to say, took place *after* Paul had written his Letters; according to modern scholarly theory, the stories were in any case assembled "backward" from the crucifixion. Yet versions of some central episodes and utterances in the life of Jesus must have been in circulation either orally or in writing from the earliest days of the sect.) In all his fairly voluminous writings, Paul virtually never mentions any of the sayings of Jesus, apart from one clear reference to the origins (in the Last Supper) of the sacraments of the bread and wine. He never directly invokes any of Jesus' addresses to the disciples or to the multitude; he never refers to the circumstances of Jesus' birth, or to his wanderings about Palestine, or to the miracles he was said to have performed; he never draws on any of the parables to illuminate his own remarks. For him, as far as the evidence of his writing goes, none of these need ever have been preserved. All he would appear to have been interested in was the crucifixion and the resurrection, and the consequences of these events, as regards both the world at large and the state of each man's soul.

In speaking or writing to certain audiences Paul invoked his Jewish past in order to demonstrate how far he had advanced from it; and to express the intimacy of the anguish he felt at the fact that all the other Jews had not done likewise. ("To the Jews," he wrote frankly in 1 Corinthians 9:20, "I became a Jew, in order to win Jews.") In trying to convince other audiences, he could be much more brusque—to put it moderately—about the Jews: ". . . who killed both the Lord Jesus and the prophets, and drove us out, and displease God, and oppose all men by hindering us from speaking to the Gentiles that they may be saved— so as always to fill up the measure of their sins. But God's wrath has come upon them at last!" (Thessalonians 1:15– 16). But whatever the tactics of his argumentation at any juncture, he never ceased proclaiming that "the curse of the Law," as he called it, had been lifted through Christ's once for all expiation of men's sins with his blood. The Jewish Law, Paul now declared, was a manifestation of pride and carnality; it was a particularly pernicious or insidious form of the general enslavement of the spirit to the body, and therefore of its enslavement to death, from which the sacrifice of Jesus had redeemed mankind. ("For the written code kills, but the Spirit gives life.") Sometimes he speaks of the Law as, at best, a discipline which the Jews had needed before the redemption offered them through Christ; at others he adopts an antinomian attitude toward it, and accuses it of positively provoking the sins which it purports to suppress; at all times, because of his emphatic if somewhat mysterious identification of the Law with "the flesh," he hails his own liberation from it as a liberation from death and corruption.

Anyway, in Paul's view the abrogation of the Law, through the "shame" of the cross, was far from being a private or parochial matter. What it meant was that the notion of the children of Abraham ("after the flesh") as the special choice and possession of their God was abrogated, too, irrevocably. So, too, was the special and exclusive covenant between them, of which the Law had been an indissoluble part. And what *that* meant was that the solitary, omnipotent God of Israel had for the first time truly become the possession not just of those whom he had previously possessed, but of all mankind. "For we hold that a man is justified by faith apart from works of law. Is God the God of Jews only? Is he not the God of Gentiles also? Yes, of Gentiles also, since God is one" (Romans 3:29).

But the concepts and the historical myths that had been the matrix of the Law, and the justification of the Law, were not abolished with it. Instead they were transposed into terms that informed and supported the new religion. The most obvious of these reformulations was that whereby the privileges enjoyed by the Israelites as God's chosen people were transferred to the new elect, the "new Israel," the new "heirs of the promise," the followers of Christ. On their behalf Paul actually went on to sharpen and generalize the doctrine of divine choice into one of outright predestination. "And those whom he predestined he also called; and those whom he called he also justified; and those whom he justified he also glorified" (Romans 8:30). There was nothing new in this, according to Paul: look how God had chosen Jacob over his twin brother when both of them were still in Rebecca's womb: "though they were not yet born and had done nothing either good or bad, in order that God's purpose of election might continue" (Romans 9:11).

Equally important was the transformation of God's "plan" in history. Oppressed, beleaguered, megalomaniac Israel had promised itself, through its prophets initially, and then through its apocalyptics, that one day its Messiah would come in power and glory to overthrow all its enemies and vindicate its God for all time. Now Paul and others said: yes, he had come, but in such humble guise that almost nobody had recognized him; in so lowly a form that the powerful and self-glorifying within Israel itself had had no compunction in destroying him. However, he would be coming again, imminently, and this time there would be no mistaking him—and no escaping him.

Which meant that within this surprising twist of the plot there lay concealed yet another. In order to bring about the great revolutions in history which had characterized his reign throughout, the God of Israel had repeatedly used evil persons, nations, and institutions as his instruments. Indeed, he had deliberately made them evil so that they could fulfil the purposes he nourished on behalf of Israel— which did not prevent him from subsequently taking his revenge on these evildoers for their misdeeds. He had hardened Pharaoh's heart, and had then punished him for not letting the children of Israel go; he had sent the Assyrian and Babylonian armies to destroy the kingdoms of Israel and Judah, and had punished them in their turn for what they had done. But on this occasion he had surpassed him-

self in ingenuity. He had used *Israel* in that very way. Israel
had been turned into his instrument to torture the good
he had sent into the world, in the form of his "Son," so
that in the end a greater good might come. But no more
than the nations he had used previously for comparable
purposes would Israel be spared the punishment it had
earned. Hence the reference (in the Letter to the Thessalonians quoted a few paragraphs above) to the Jews acting as
they do *"so as* . . . to fill up the measure of their sins"—
a theme which recurs in various forms in each of the Gospels. "The Son of man," Jesus says of Judas Iscariot in Matthew (26:24), "goes as it is written of him, but woe to
that man by whom the Son of man is betrayed." And woe
to the people whose name Judas bore.

The covenant and the kingdom-to-come had to be wholly
depoliticized and denationalized; they were transformed
into images of inward states of being, or into descriptions
of the fellowship of the church, or into anticipations of
the blessings of the hereafter; or all three at once. The relatively recent but widespread acceptance among the Jews
of Palestine of the doctrines of the afterlife, and of eternal
rewards and punishments, made this kind of "spiritualiza-
tion" of the promises in the Hebrew Scriptures more persuasive than it might otherwise have been. The Christians were
not the inventors of the retrospectively allegorical and metaphorical readings of the Scriptures which such beliefs demanded: apocalyptics and sectarians like those in Qumran,
and Jewish philosophers like Philo, as well as scores of
learned midrashic expounders and explicators of the texts,
had pioneered the way. However, the expectation of spiritual rewards in the next world had always coexisted among
the Jews with their hopes of a restored political kingdom;
any final redemption that did not at some stage include

an earthly Jerusalem restored to the faithful was inconceivable to them. Now the Christians offered their elect—composed as it was of individual souls united only by faith—not a land and sovereignty over it, as Yahweh had done to his chosen people, but membership of a church: this being interpreted as membership both of a human fraternity and of the mystical body of Christ. "We, though many, are one body in Christ, and individually members of one another" (Romans 12:5).

Why the God who had first revealed himself to Israel should have taken this way rather than some other in order to make himself accessible to all mankind; why the sufferings endured by a preexistent divine redeemer, incarnated as the Son, should be supposed to have the effect of canceling out the sins of all past and future generations; why aspects of the world or categories within it as dissimilar as sin, death, and flesh, and the Jewish Law should turn out to be virtually indistinguishable from one another—these are questions it is impossible to answer in terms of "the story of the stories," and its transmutations, which are my subject. However, the story does have a direct bearing on two interconnected issues or complexes of feeling arising from those questions. The first is the relationship between the sacrifice made by Christ on the cross and the sacrifices offered to the God of Israel in the Temple. This is a recurring theme for reflection and comparison in the Christian Scriptures; not least in the Letters of Paul, once again. The second has to do with the nature of Paul's "release" from the Jewish Law.

In the Letters to the Hebrews (usually considered to be not one of Paul's own Letters, incidentally, but a document emerging from a Pauline "school"), Christ's sacrifice is described as the apocalyptic culmination and replacement of the sacrifices previously made by the Israelites to Yahweh. "He [Christ] has no need like those high priests to offer sacrifices daily . . . he has appeared once for all *at the end of the age* to put away sin by the sacrifice of himself" (7:27; 9:26). Christ accomplishes this through the power given to him as "the Son of God." As "the Son," who has taken on human flesh, and the human capacity to feel pain, he is able to make expiation to "the Father" for the sins committed by all men. ("For . . . we are reconciled to God by the death of his Son"—Romans 5:10.) Now, even if the familial relationship implied in the "Sonship" is regarded as nothing more than a metaphor or symbol for the mysterious unity and self-division of the godhead, Christ's sacrifice is nevertheless clearly presented as one in which a "father" permits or demands the immolation of his "child."

Turn now to the Hebrew Scriptures. There child sacrifice is mentioned many times: always as an abomination. It is spoken of as one of the vilest practices of the nations surrounding Israel; as something for which Yahweh is ever ready to punish his people (by exile and various other, familiar torments) whenever they are tempted toward it. There must be a score of denunciations of the practice, in its various forms, in lawbooks like Leviticus (18:21; 20:2–5) and Deuteronomy (12:31); in the prophecies of the Second Isaiah (57:5), Jeremiah (19:5, 32–35, etc.), Micah (6:7), and Ezekiel (20:26, 23:39, etc.); and in the Psalms (106:37–38). Most, but not all, of these are references to parents sacrificing their children by fire. The very intensity of the denunciations no doubt reveals more of the writers' motives and misgivings than they were wholly aware of. Presumably they had good reason to suspect that a god, any god, including perhaps one or more of those precursors or rivals whom Yahweh had "taken over," might be gratified by the degree of devotion revealed in such an act. Though there is only one outright instance of Israelite child sacrifice in the Hebrew Scriptures—that of Jephthah's daughter in Judges—they contain many "surrogates" for it, or sublimated versions of it. The binding of Isaac at Yahweh's behest is one; probably the most famous and most often misinterpreted of all. Another is the collocation in Exodus of the slaughter of the Egyptian firstborn on the night of the first Passover, the demand by Yahweh that in return for this deed all firstborn Israelite males should be "consecrated" to him in perpetuity, and the sacrifice of a lamb "without blemish" by each Israelite family on the night of that and every subsequent Passover. The rite of circumcision itself, in my view, belongs on the list. But all this does not diminish—on the contrary, it reinforces—the sense one has of a profound recoil against the offering of children as a sacrifice pleasing to God, and of the urgency of the need that was felt to tempt as well as threaten the people from falling (back?) into the practice.

And yet here is Paul, by his own account brought up in the Law as a zealous Pharisee, announcing that "we" are reconciled to "God the Father" by the death of his "Son"! (Whom he also compares, incidentally, to the paschal lamb.) One would have thought that so striking an example of "the return of the repressed" would have caught Freud's attention in his examination of the biblical texts in *Moses and Monotheism*; but he makes no mention of it. The theory of the Christian sacrifice which Freud puts forward involves a great variety of improbabilities: among them a "primal horde" of sons and brothers (in an Israelite version) murdering Moses, the father and founder of the religion, and then later deifying him; a thousand-year "latency period" in the history of the race, paralleling that between infancy and puberty in the biography of an individual; the rediscovery by Paul of this primeval crime; his proposed expiation of it by the death of Christ, acting as the symbolical or reincarnated "leader" of the original, murderous, youthful horde . . . and so forth.

My speculations, I can claim, are governed by what actually appears in the text. It does not seem to me in the least fanciful, especially in view of Paul's own insistence on the continuity as well as the difference between the two testaments or covenants, to juxtapose the prohibitions against child sacrifice in the Jewish Law and the celebration in the Christian Scriptures of the willing sacrifice of a "Son" (innocent, without blemish) to his "God and Father." Nor does it seem to me extravagant to note that it is Paul himself, a man intimate with the Jewish Law, who is the very first to see a particular historic event in these terms; and who hails this sacrifice, which the Hebrew Scriptures would have regarded as an atrocity, as an eternally efficacious atonement for the guilt and sin of all mankind, and hence as an apocalyptic liberation from the Law.*

And the conclusion to be drawn from all this: other than that "the repressed" in one form or another will always "return"? Well, one conclusion might be that Paul's liberation from the Law was not so much a consequence of his faith in Christ, as he repeatedly seems to suggest, but rather

---

* As a result of a characteristic process of interpretation and inversion, the binding of Isaac became not only a "type" of the sacrifice of Christ, but also an illustration of the inherent malevolence and bloodthirstiness of the Jews and their God. The story was seen as a description of how Abraham/Yahweh/Judaism sought unsuccessfully to destroy the infant Isaac/Christ/Christianity. This interpretation depended on the (post-scriptural) teachings whereby Christ the Son in effect displaced, or at least became "consubstantial" with, God the Father as the supreme object of Christian worship.

a precondition of that faith. Only a man who had already revolted against the Law would have been able to see Christ's death on the cross as an oblation by the "Son" which the God of Israel would find welcome. Indeed, the argument can be taken further: among the guilts from which Paul's vision of Christ redeemed him was, precisely and paradoxically, the guilt he felt about his inner abandonment of the Law.

But then, Paul virtually said as much, in writing of the way in which the Law goaded him into sin by its very existence. "If it had not been for the law, I should not have known sin. I should not have known what it was to covet, if the law had not said, 'You shall not covet'" (Romans 7:7). In other words, the demand for obedience which the Law made was also an irresistible, shameful, secret challenge to disobedience. What a relief, then, to be able to proclaim publicly that the Law was dead; that it had been superseded; that by virtue of his newfound faith, and the grace that had come upon him as a result, he was no longer bound to it! His Letters speak of this relief with an intensity that is remarkable even by his standards. (They speak of it with great frequency, too.) From that alone one can guess how weary he had become of his obligation to uphold and fulfill the Law, or to seem to do so: if it is possible to speak of weariness as a passion, that is the passion, one might guess, which possessed his soul as he set out on the road to Damascus.

The great convulsion he went through should not be understood, however, solely in terms of the contradictions and ambivalences of his own standing in relation to the Law. The contradictions he perceived within the Law as an institution, as a historic fact, appear to have been equally intolerable to him. This is as much as to say that he found intolerable the contradictions inherent in his people's history and its conception of its God. Of that his writings give ample evidence: both directly in their hunger for universality, in his eagerness to reach out to the world; and indirectly in their related ambition to achieve logical or systematic coherence. Paul was a Jew of the diaspora. He grew up as a Roman citizen, in a Greek-speaking environment, among a variety of Near Eastern peoples following a variety of creeds, many of them forms or syntheses of one another. Inevitably he was familiar with the cults, myths, and mysteries that accompanied them. He also had an acquaintance with the Greek philosophical tradition, and the modes of speculation and logical argumentation developed within it. None of this means that he was an "assimilated" Jew. Even if some of his claims about his grounding in the Jewish tradition were made for rhetorical effect, the depth of his engagement with the Jewish past cannot be doubted. Nor can one doubt that he found it impossible to reconcile the claims of that past with what he saw around him.

Election, the Law, the covenant, the promises, and the history were all one. They spoke of God—and God spoke of himself—as the sole creator of the world and of everyone in it. No less loudly and firmly did they speak of Israel as his special concern: compared to Israel, to whom alone he had given his Law, all other nations and their interests were subordinate. But were they? Why were they not? What could make them so? How could the mighty Roman empire, and the Parthians on its eastern border, and the Greeks, and the Egyptians, and a score of other peoples, become subject to Israel and the God of Israel? And if they did, what then? If Yahweh was the governor of the whole world, and his Law was the absolute, unalterable good he declared it to be, why had the Jews been the only people to be blessed and (in Paul's most private experience of it) to be tormented by it? Either the world as it existed, in which the Jews were a poor, inconsequential, scattered race, with their homeland occupied yet again by yet another foreign conqueror, was an affront to God; or else God as he had hitherto been conceived was an affront to the world. Which one of these was it?

We know how these questions were resolved by Paul. He took to himself another affront, the "scandal" and "shame" of the cross, and the triumph of the resurrection which he believed to have come out of it, and made his way with it, or through it, into another world: one which he was sure would last for a brief period only, before Christ returned and Paul's own actions would be justified eternally and universally. "We know that the whole creation has been groaning in travail together until now; and not only the creation, but we ourselves, who have the first fruits of the Spirit" (Romans 8:22–23). Only by his leaving behind him his people and their Law, the old covenant and the unfulfilled promises, could the world be won and the promises fulfilled.

> For there is no distinction between Jew and Greek; the same Lord is Lord of all and bestows his riches upon all who call upon him. For, 'every one who calls upon the name of the Lord will be saved.'
> But how are men to call upon him in whom they have not believed? And how are they to believe in him of whom they have never heard? And how are they to hear without a preacher? And how can men preach unless they are sent?
>
> ROMANS 10:12–15

There is nothing remotely like the Gospels in the Hebrew Scriptures or in the extra-canonical literature of the period. No doubt it is true that the ethical teachings of Jesus have their roots in the prophetic, apocalyptic, and Pharisaic traditions with which he was familiar. (Scholars have long since abandoned the idea that his ethics can only be understood in opposition to those of Pharisaism.) It is also true that Josephus's account of the Roman occupation of Judea positively bristles, as it were, with crucifixes bearing the bodies of those who died for their nation and their beliefs. Two of them, dismissed in characteristic fashion by the Gospel writers as "robbers" and "criminals," may have died alongside Jesus. None of this, however, affects the singularity and the poignance of the impression made by the Gospels—an impression which springs both from the overall rapidity and purposefulness of the narratives, and from the vividness of the incidents, images, and parables within them. In fact, one of the most remarkable features of the story as a whole is that the patently mythical elements in it render the sufferings of the individual at its heart even more painful to read about than they might otherwise have been. After all, the various myths which his life and death are made to illustrate are as much an expression of human impulse as are his teachings, or indeed as are the tortures which were inflicted on him.

There is ample evidence in the Gospels, and in what is known from other sources about Palestine under the Romans, to suggest that Jesus was executed as a Jewish troublemaker; as a man who had, or was reputed by his followers to have, messianic and hence (from the Roman point of view) revolutionary pretensions. In carrying out this deed, the Romans were at least helped, if not positively provoked, by Jewish sacerdotal officials, who held their positions by grace of the country's colonial masters, and were anxious not to have the *status quo* disturbed by trouble in the streets—both because they wanted to protect their own positions; and because they foresaw (rightly, as events were to show during the rebellion against Rome, a few decades later) the consequences of messianic enthusiasm among the populace.*

So the man was done to death. Thereupon his death became an instrument with which to malign and torment generation after generation of Jews. It also became the means by which some of the most grandiose visions of the Hebrew prophets were realized. Because of the interpretation Paul had placed on his life and death, the words of Jesus, and the words of the prophets, and the idea of the single, transcendent God of Israel, were eventually, at the cost of much blood and effort, carried to the ends of the earth.

---

* There is a passage in the Gospel of John which throws a shadow across a particularly horrific series of episodes in twentieth-century history. "If we let him [Jesus] go on thus," the council of "chief priests and Pharisees" is reported as saying, "every one will believe in him, and the Romans will come and destroy both our holy place and our nation." Whereupon the high priest Caiaphas is said to declare it "expedient" that "one man should die for the people, and that the whole nation should not perish." Words like these were actually uttered, hopelessly enough, during the Nazi occupation of Europe by certain Jewish leaders who were compelled to choose who among their people should be driven on to the "transports" to the death camps. ("To ensure that at least a remnant of Jews survive," one of them said, "I myself had to lead Jews to death.") Some of those leaders were bewildered, well-meaning nobodies; a few were near-madmen, who reveled in the power of life and death that had been thrust upon them; most were (or began as) honorable and responsible men who tried to protect the people supposedly under their charge from the maniacal fury that was turned against them. All of them imagined that by sending some innocent victims to the gas chambers, as they were told to do, they might be able to save others. All of them were wrong.

CHAPTER FOURTEEN

FORWARD AND BACK

The religion of Israel was centered on the idea of a people to whom a transcendent, solitary God had made a special revelation of himself and of his Law, and upon whom, as a mark of his favor, he had bestowed a territorial and political identity. These elements were transmitted to Orthodox Judaism in different ways: the first directly, together with a greatly enlarged body of Law; the second in an enlarged yet also in a somewhat attenuated form, as a memory of the past, as a hope for the future, and even as a vaguely conceived presaging of the world to come.

This idealized recollection and expectation of sovereignty by the people of Israel over a particular geographical location, however vaguely or grandiosely it was defined, was a source of strength for Judaism. But it also put a tether on its "reach." The worldwide enlargements of the scope of Yahweh's power with which the prophets had striven to glorify him, and which the apocalyptics had reinterpreted in their cosmic fashion, were in effect bound to put more and more strain on everything in the religion that remained purely local or parochial, limited geographically and nationally. (Though this was far from the intention of either the prophetic or the apocalyptic writers.) It is paradoxical that the avowedly political-territorial strain in Judaism, which has always figured so luridly in the paranoias of the anti-Semites, made it certain that "world domination" would never be a real prospect for the religion; certainly not a prospect of the kind that it became for both Christianity and Islam, the daughter religions of Israel.

The history of Judaism as a proselytizing creed in the Greco-Roman era—the one period during which it apparently developed a strong urge to gain converts from the heathen peoples of the empire—illustrates this point. Large numbers of converts, according to the historians, were won over; some of them were forcibly converted by the Hasmonean rulers of Judea, before the Romans put astop to their policy of territorial expansion. What brought the proselytizing movement to an end throughout the empire, however, was the impatient messianism and nationalism of the Jews in Palestine and elsewhere who could not bear to see the Romans ruling over Jerusalem. They kept the city and the countryside around it in a constant state of turmoil; they (in all likelihood a group of extreme Jewish Christians among them) disturbed the peace in Rome itself; finally they rose up in outright rebellion against the imperial forces in the homeland, their faith in the God of Israel encouraging them to disregard the heavy odds against the success of the enterprise. It failed, of course, amid great carnage; and irrevocably envenomed the ever-uneasy relations between Jews and Romans. (One consequence of this was the destruction of the original Jewish Christian community in Jerusalem: which meant that the revised, Pauline, "Gentilized" version of Christianity alone survived.) Thus a political-territorial upheaval, expressive of one aspiration of Judaism, destroyed a great historic opportunity—Judaism's "moment," as Ernest Renan called it*—expressive of another of its aspirations. Nothing like that moment has recurred since; or is likely to recur.

Both these aspects of the religion are inalienable from it; they are also difficult to reconcile with one another. The fact is that while monolatry is inherently expansionist—for the one God must fill up with all the force of his authority the space that becomes available to him, if he is to remain one, and without rivals—nationalism, ethnicity, and sovereignty are concepts which have meaning only in terms of limitation, of exclusion and separation. The same is true *a fortiori* of the concept of chosenness. The most common line among Jewish apologists in attempting to resolve the contradiction is to invoke in some form the idea of Israel as the "kingdom of priests" referred to in Exodus; and the promise to Abraham in Genesis that all nations would eventually "bless themselves" through him. Such statements, it is claimed, point forward to the day when, in Zephaniah's words, all peoples will call in a "pure language . . . on the name of God and serve him with one accord" (3:9); or when, as Isaiah puts it (11:9), "the earth shall be full of the knowledge of God as the waters cover the sea." How is the transition to be made? How is a jealously preserved separateness and particularity to lead to this kind of unanimity and fullness? Not, it would be argued, through the seeking out of proselytes; still less through the attempt to establish any form of political dominance over other nations. Rather, it will come about by force of example, by the demonstration in history and beyond it of the value of the covenant; a demonstration which

---

* Quoted by Salo W. Baron in *A Social and Religious History of the Jews,* Volume I.

would ultimately bring other peoples, each in its own way, to the God who had initiated all history.

However difficult or obscure this doctrine may appear to nonbelievers, it is important to Judaism, and hence to believing Jews. It must be said, though, that one can find only a fairly limited number of undeveloped hints at it in the Scriptures themselves (Deuteronomy and the prophets included). There, for reasons I have tried to outline, and in a manner I have tried to describe, the universality of God is primarily seen as a means of furthering his preoccupation with Israel; and not, so to speak, vice versa. It follows that the biblical writers are not really concerned with trying to explain how or why the separateness from all others of Israel in blood, belief, and daily practice—a separateness imposed upon them by their God, and zealously maintained by a fine, all-embracing, God-given network of taboos and restrictions—should serve the end of bringing those others *willingly* to worship God; nor why the restoration, under Yahweh, of Israel's sovereignty over a particular portion of the globe should be an absolute *sine qua non* for the establishment among all nations both of universal peace and of the truth about the nature of the divinity.

Pauline Christianity, by contrast, took over the expansionist or universal deity, and (as it were) expanded with him, untrammeled by any contradictory, centrifugal pull toward nationhood. The distinction made by the church between the elect and the damned, the saved and the lost, the faithful and the infidel, was, according to Paul, to be based on grounds of belief only; no one was to be excluded from its ranks because of his blood or birthplace or political condition. Thus the logic of the Christian position, under its all-embracing God, was clear; and Christian writers have never been loath to condemn Judaism both because of its illogicality and because of its alleged selfishness or narrowness, compared with what they claim to be the universal appeal and the universal charity of the Christian message. The separatism of the Jews has generally been characterized by Christian writers as a natural complement to the proud, cold-blooded, self-regarding "legalism" which they impute to the Jewish religion, the Jewish God, and the Jewish character.

However, *in principle* Christians who uphold the church's traditional teachings have to accept that for a universal God to choose a particular people to be his favorites, and to reveal himself to them while denying his presence to others, and to give them a special dispensation of laws of great significance to himself, and to confer on them specific, localized political and territorial advantages over other peoples, as the Jews claimed he did in his dealings with them—that all this is an entirely reasonable and appropriate way for him to have proceeded. They have to accept this proposition simply because the entire Pauline system is based on Christianity's "inheriting" the promises made by Yahweh to the Israelites; it could not have done this had his promises to them, and his accompanying demands of them, not been regarded as good, reasonable, justifiable promises and demands, worthy in every respect of a universal God. The fact that the Jews subsequently proved themselves unworthy of his trust, and even the fact that he had always known that they would so prove themselves, and would thus unwittingly fulfill the plan he had prepared for all mankind, does not affect his right to have approached the Israelites as he did, and to have cultivated them, and to have used them in a manner that distinguished them from and beyond all others.

In effect, the Christians find themselves committed to

the uncomfortable doctrine that choice and favoritism on the part of God—and their manifestations in nationhood, political sovereignty, territorial enlargements and abridgments, and private legal or juridical arrangements between himself and his chosen people—were proper to his nature and indispensable to his *modus operandi* until the eschatological moment of Christ's birth, death, and resurrection. Thereafter these selfsame features of the religion of Israel and of the Jews ceased to be divinely inspired and hence commendable . . . and became instead narrowly selfish, illogical, legalistic, unspiritual, earthly, provincial, and so forth. But the difference between the two religions in these respects would appear to be essentially one of timing, rather than one of logic or some ultimate principle involving the dignity of the deity and the breadth of his concern for mankind. Christians must acknowledge that it was once mysteriously all right for God to have behaved in this fashion, but ceased to be so at a decisive trans-historical moment; Orthodox Jews say it is still all right for him to mark them out for special favor, at the very least until his ultimate purposes for mankind are revealed—and preferably thereafter as well; a nonbeliever might ask how or why the moral nature of the creator of the universe should be supposed, one way or the other, to be subject to alteration in time.

It is extraordinary that a theology as systematic and coherent as Paul's should turn out to rest so heavily on a series of entirely arbitrary or axiomatic premises about the relationship between the "old" covenant described and enacted in the Hebrew Scriptures and the "new" covenant which he was inspired to adumbrate. The fact that Paul was not among those who had known Jesus in the flesh was, one must suspect, of critical significance in this regard. (He was an apostle, as he says, "not from man nor through men.")

That was what gave him the freedom to deal as he did with concepts like chosenness, promise, circumcision, the Law, the sacrificial system, and the rest; and to proffer through Christ his own spiritualized or universalized version of each. However, the point I want to make here is not that the premises of Paul's theology are ultimately as "private" to him as the vision he had of Jesus on the road to Damascus (however systematically he may have developed what he believed to be the implications of both). Rather it is that *any* revealed religion, no matter how generalized and world-encompassing its claims and ambitions, will have to base itself on various manifestations of an unexplained and inexplicable favoritism on the part of the deity. He has to choose just a few out of an infinite number of moments in history in which to reveal himself, preferably (though not always) through highly public displays of his presence; he has to choose one person or small groups of persons before whom such displays will take place; he has to choose one or more geographical locations for his initial, faith-generating appearances.

The idea that a "God or Nature" (to use the Spinozist formula), which makes manifest everywhere the regularity and mutual dependence of the laws which sustain it in existence, should seek to reveal what is morally most significant to all mankind by miraculously suspending, abrogating, or absconding from its own laws—this idea has long been regarded by many as a stumbling block rather than a source of faith. Virgin births, partings of the water, witherings of fig trees, and so forth are felt to be a derogation from the dignity of the divine, not an addition to it. Something of the same sort, for many people, applies to the idea that a revelation like the one described above should be vouchsafed only at one particular time, in one particular place, to one particular group—all others having to take it on faith or by repute thereafter. Of course, not all men are equally gifted spiritually or intellectually; some have far more to teach us than others; history suggests that the same may be true of entire cultures and epochs. But that is an observation about human beings, not about some "arrangement" external to them to which they respond. Again, to say, as a devout Christian would, that each of us crucifies Christ daily through our sins, and that the crucifixion is an event therefore that takes place throughout history; and that the same is true of the resurrection, which is rehearsed whenever men overcome pain, or despair, or their own evil impulses, by attending to Christ; or to say, as Orthodox Jews do, that all the generations of Israel stood together with Moses at Sinai to receive the Law—none of this really meets the problem of a unique, unrepeatable intervention or irruption by "God or Nature" in its own mundane dimensions of time and space; it is merely to assert in another way the importance of that intervention. To the skeptic, "God or Nature," if it is to be true to itself, must present itself on morally equal terms for examination by men of different generations (however ill or well placed they may be to take advantage of their opportunities); if it does not appear to do so, then what we are examining is not it, but ourselves—our traditions, our systems of belief and explanation.

But then, I have already made clear my conviction that one of the remarkable things about the Hebrew Scriptures is not so much the idea of God choosing Israel for his own, and the description of the ways in which he makes his choice manifest, but the profoundly energizing uneasiness about the moral implications of the entire process which the story reveals overall. In its way that seems to me quite as original, and as provocative, morally speaking, as what the story tells us of the qualities that enable God to exercise choice: his invisibility, his transcendence, and his solitude.

To a skeptical reader the Hebrew and Christian Scriptures remain a unique revelation only in the most obvious sense: as a revelation of the minds of particular and extraordinary men in a sequence of times and places. Because of their cumulative nature, they are also a wonderful illustration of the nature of a tradition. Through them and in them we can see how every generation understands its own predicaments in the light of the assumptions and expectations it has inherited from the past; and how the past that is "inherited" is in turn rewritten and understood anew in the light of current predicaments. Even beyond this, however, the Scriptures are a revelation of how mysterious and terrible a place the world can appear to be, as a moral and physical fact, to those who open themselves wholly to it. As we read, we do not know whether to wonder more at the God they present in all his different manifestations, or at the men whose minds and imaginations made room for him.

All that said, it is impossible for a skeptic to go through the Scriptures without feeling a wonder of quite another kind, as well. When one thinks of the incalculable influence these writings have had, still have, and will continue to have on the course of world history in the foreseeable future; when one thinks more or less at random of the wars that have been fought over them, of the worlds conquered for them, of the works of art inspired by them; of the massacres and martyrdoms arising from them that have taken place in the heart of Europe during our own century, or of the state of Israel grappling today with its neighbors over the ancient sites, or of Protestants and Catholics trying to burn each other out of their homes in Northern Ireland, or of the pilgrims flying in jumbo jets to Mecca, or of Poles and Bolivian peasants turning for help to Rome—one is likely, then, to be overwhelmed not by the power of the Scriptures but by a sense of their frailty. Is it possible that *these* are the stories behind all that movement and passion? How could the evident confusions and illogicalities of the over-arching story of the Hebrew Scriptures have had so great an effect on so many people? How could the patent contrivances of Paul, in substituting on the strength of his own say-so one set of divine demands and promises for another, have been so persuasive worldwide? Is it really possible? Has one read the same texts as all those men and women who have lived within and (many of them) died for their faiths?

A believer—even one who believes that it is only through the medium of myth that we can apprehend a supernatural reality which is both personal and yet untranslatable into human terms—would answer directly: No, you have not read the same text, because you have read it without faith. One implication of this reply, oddly enough, is that it is not what we read that generates the faith, but the faith that generates what we read. (There is a great deal of truth in this; but it does not exclude another and equally important truth: that both believer and nonbeliever can agree about many things of prime importance in the text they have shared.) Such a believer might also claim that it is precisely the disproportion of which I have complained between the "frailty" of the stories and their immeasurable consequences that reveals them to have been divinely inspired. The inconsistencies in the Hebrew Scriptures are nothing more, in terms of this argument, than those which will inevitably arise when a pristine revelation is falteringly transcribed by fallible men; the "contrivances" of Paul are not his, but those of his Master; or if another way of putting it is preferred, they are the direct result of the Gospel preachings, and of the crucifixion and resurrection myth, doing their work through the medium of Paul's uniquely speculative and poetic imagination. *They* are primary; they are what I have unwisely called his "say-so."

Well, in the end one has to fall back on that mode of understanding and explanation which most satisfies one's sense of what kind of place the world actually is. And it is here, if anywhere, that the inadequacy of the assumptions on which I set out on this task becomes most obvious: the inadequacy, that is, of reading these stories *as* stories. However imaginatively compelling they may be as narratives, they have never existed solely as such. They do not belong merely between the covers of a book, or in the minds of individual readers. Having grown out of a variety of cults, they have been formalized into divine services and liturgies of great power and elaborateness; rooted in custom and community, they have been an integral part of the public lives of nations and their institutions; they have been transmitted from generation to generation, among the most intimate and least easily surrendered continuities of family life; they have been turned into brick and stone, pigment, music, bodies of learning, literature, folk tale, and (not least) the common speech of people who may not even recall the origin of some of the words and images they habitually use. That is how they have come to exercise so extraordinary a power over the internal and external development of an entire civilization.

And that isn't all. The skeptic or rationalist or naturalist who registers his surprise at the disparity (in his terms)

between the content of the stories and the effects they have
had should make a real job of his skepticism; he should
turn it against himself. Does he really propose to set it
up as the highest of all human values? The court of last
appeal? What is there in history to make him suppose that
coherence, orderliness, or the capacity to withstand a rigor-
ously skeptical intellectual analysis are either desirable or
necessary qualities in the myths that move men to belief
and action? Isn't there a great deal in history which shows
the exact opposite to be the case?

After all, I have argued that it was the *un*truth of the
prophetic interpretation of the history of Israel which en-
sured its survival; and hence the survival of the Jews as a
group; and hence the birth of Christianity. Given that degree
of perverse cunning on the part of history, it should not
come as a surprise that it is precisely the confusion and
incoherence of the various elements which make up "the
story of the stories" in the Hebrew Scriptures, and the patently wishful fantasies of restoration and domination with
which it concludes, that have been seen by the anti-Semites
as infallible evidence of sinister, world-encompassing de-
signs on the part of the Jews. Nor should it come as a
surprise that the message of peace and loving-kindness to
be found in the Gospels is inextricably embedded in a po-
lemic of (literally) murderous hostility against the people
to whom Jesus belonged. But then, the contents of his message probably owe something to the fact that the Gospel
writers deliberately depoliticized—for political reasons!—
the messiahdom imputed to Jesus by his original followers.
As a result they succeeded in transforming the whole story
into a morality tale with an irresistible and universal dramatic appeal. The priests, the Pharisees, and the Jewish
mob oppose Jesus for no other reason, essentially, than that

he is good and they are bad; he is weak and virtually alone, they are powerful and many; he preaches peace, and they put their trust in cruelty and violence. Their triumph is complete. Then comes the resurrection.

A few pages ago (and elsewhere, too), I said that the Scriptures provide us with a wonderful example of the growth of a tradition; of its power over a period of a thousand years and more to help men shape their experience into patterns comprehensible to them, and thus to help sustain them, as individuals and in communities, in the face of the adversities which time never fails to bring. All that is true. Yet who could have imagined that within (let's say) the song of triumph over the Egyptians in Exodus, with its celebration of Yahweh's deliverance from slavery of his chosen people, there lay concealed the potentiality of Israel's Messiah rising from his cross in order (according to other celebrants) to make manifest all mankind's deliverance from sin? If we try to look forward rather than back, it may seem that we should be most impressed not by the continuity of the story but by its wild unpredictability; by the plethora of opportunities in it for everything to have turned out differently.

Can these two points of view—looking forward, and looking back—be reconciled? In life, no. But every story we tell each other, including this one, which I have told about the biblical story, is an attempt to achieve just such a reconciliation.

SELECT BIBLIOGRAPHY

Albright, W. F., *The Biblical Period from Abraham to Ezra*. New York, 1963.
———, *From the Stone Age to Christianity*. Baltimore, 1957.
Allegro, J., *The Dead Sea Scrolls: A Reappraisal*. Harmondsworth, 1978.
Baron, S. W., *A Social and Religious History of the Jews*. Volume I: *Ancient Times*. New York, 1952.
Brandon, S. G. F., *Jesus and the Zealots*. Manchester, 1967.
Bultmann, R., *Theology of the New Testament*. Translated by K. Grobel. London, 1978.
Charles, R. H., ed., *The Apocrypha and Pseudepigrapha of the Old Testament in English*. Oxford, 1979.
Cook, S. A., *An Introduction to the Bible*. Harmondsworth, 1954.
Cornford, F. M., *Greek Religious Thought*. London, 1923.
Dodd, C. H., *The Meaning of Paul for Today*. London, 1978.
Driver, S. R., *Introduction to the Literature of the Old Testament*. Edinburgh, 1898.
Eichrodt, W., *Theology of the Old Testament*. Translated by J. Baker. London, 1957.
Eissfeldt, O., *The Old Testament: An Introduction*. Translated by P. R. Ackroyd. Oxford, 1974.
The Encyclopaedia Britannica. Chicago and London, 1963.
The Encyclopaedia Judaica. Jerusalem, 1972.
The Encyclopaedia of Religion and Ethics. Edinburgh, 1911.
Epstein, I., *Judaism*. London, 1977.
Feuerbach, L., *The Essence of Christianity*. Translated by Marian Evans. New York, 1957.
Frankfort, H., *Kingship and the Gods*. Chicago, 1978.
Frankfort, H. & H. A., *et al.*, *Before Philosophy*. Harmondsworth, 1967.

Freud, S., *Moses and Monotheism.* Translated by K. Jones. London, 1954.

Fuller, R., *The Foundations of New Testament Christology.* London, 1979.

Gaster, T. H., *Thespis.* New York, 1950.

Ginsburg, L., *Legends of the Bible.* Abridged. New York, 1956.

Grayzel, S., *A History of the Jews.* New York, 1968.

Heaton, E. W., *Everyday Life in Old Testament Times.* London, 1966.

Hegel, G. W. F., *Werke.* Band I: *Frühe Schriften.* Frankfurt, 1971.

Herder, J. G., *Sämmtliche Werke.* Band XII. Berlin, 1878.

Heschel, A. J., *The Prophets.* New York, 1962.

Hobbes, T., *Leviathan.* Harmondsworth, 1978.

Hooke, S. H., *Middle Eastern Mythology.* London, 1968.

James, E. O., *The Ancient Gods.* London, 1967.

Johnson, P., *A History of Christianity.* Harmondsworth, 1978.

Josephus, F., *The Jewish War.* Translated by G. A. Williamson. Harmondsworth, 1959.

Kaufmann, Y., *The Religion of Israel.* Translated and abridged by M. Greenberg. New York, 1972.

Kermode, F., *The Genesis of Secrecy.* Oxford, 1980.

Klausner, J., *Jesus of Nazareth.* Translated by H. Danby. London, 1925.

————, *The Messianic Idea in Israel.* Translated by W. F. Stinespring. London, 1956.

Kitchin, H. A., *Ancient Orient and Old Testament.* London, 1966.

Lawrence, D. H., *Apocalypse and the Writings on Revelation.* Edited by M. Kalnins. Cambridge, 1980.

Leach, E., *Genesis as Myth and Other Essays.* London, 1969.

Luckenbill, D. D., *Ancient Records of Assyria and Babylon.* Chicago, 1927.

Mendenhall, G. E., *Law and Covenant in Israel and the Ancient Near East.* Pittsburgh, 1955.

Moore, G. F., *Judaism in the First Centuries of the Christian Era.* New York, 1974.

Mowinckel, S., *He That Cometh.* Translated by G. W. Anderson. Oxford, 1956.

Neitzsche, F., *The Anti-Christ.* Translated by W. Kaufmann. New York, 1960.

Noth, M., *The History of Israel.* London, 1976.

Oppenheim, A. L., *Ancient Mesopotamia.* Chicago, 1977.

Perrin, N., *The New Testament: An Introduction.* New York, 1974.

Pritchard, J. B., ed., *The Ancient Near Eastern Texts Relating to the Old Testament.* Third edition. Princeton, 1969.

Robinson, H. W., *Religious Ideas of the Old Testament.* London, 1964.

Rowley, H. H., *The Biblical Doctrine of Election*. London, 1950.
_____, *Worship in Ancient Israel*. London, 1967.
Schechter, S., *Aspects of Rabbinic Theology*. New York, 1961.
Scholem, G., *The Messianic Idea in Judaism*. New York, 1974.
Schweitzer, A., *The Quest of the Historical Jesus*. Translated by W. Montgomery. London, 1964.
Simon, M., and Freedman, H., eds., *The Midrash Rabbah: Genesis and Exodus*. Translated by the editors. London, 1939.
Smith, G. A., *The Historical Geography of the Holy Land*. London, 1974.
Spinoza, B., *A Theologico-Political Treatise*. Translated by R. H. M. Elwes. New York, 1974.
Vermes, G., *The Dead Sea Scrolls in English*. Harmondsworth, 1979.
_____, *Jesus the Jew*. London, 1973.
Voegelin, E., *Israel and Revelation*. Baton Rouge, 1976.
Von Rad, G., *Old Testament Theology*. Translated by D. M. G. Stalker. London, 1979.
Vriezen, T. C., *The Religion of Ancient Israel*. London, 1967.
Weber, M., *Ancient Judaism*. Translated by H. Garth and D. Martindale. London, 1969.
_____, *The Sociology of Religion*. Translated by E. Fischoff. London, 1965.
Weil, S., *Waiting on God*. London, 1973.
Weiler, G., *Jewish Theocracy*. Tel Aviv, 1973.
Wellhausen, J., *Prolegomena to the History of Israel*. Translated by J. S. Black and A. Menzies. Edinburgh, 1885.
Winter, P., *On the Trial of Jesus*. Berlin, 1961.